A TRANSFORMATIVE READING OF THE BIBLE

A Transformative
READING OF THE BIBLE

Explorations of
Holistic Human Transformation

Yung Suk Kim

CASCADE *Books* • Eugene, Oregon

A TRANSFORMATIVE READING OF THE BIBLE
Explorations of Holistic Human Transformation

Copyright © 2013 Yung Suk Kim. All rights reserved. Except for brief quotations in critical publications or reviews, no part of this book may be reproduced in any manner without prior written permission from the publisher. Write: Permissions, Wipf and Stock Publishers, 199 W. 8th Ave., Suite 3, Eugene, OR 97401.

Cascade Books
An Imprint of Wipf and Stock Publishers
199 W. 8th Ave., Suite 3
Eugene, OR 97401

www.wipfandstock.com

ISBN 13:978-1-62032-221-5

Cataloging-in-Publication data:

Kim, Yung Suk

A transformative reading of the bible : explorations of holistic human transformation / Yung Suk Kim.

p. ; cm. — Includes bibliographical references and index(es).

ISBN 13: 978-1-62032-221-5

1. Bible—Study and teaching. 2. Bible—Criticism, interpretation, etc. I. Title.

BS600.3 K45 2013

Manufactured in the U.S.A.

I will put my law within them, and I will write it on their hearts; and I will be their God, and they shall be my people
(Jeremiah 31:33)

Do not be conformed to this world, but be transformed by the renewing of your minds, so that you may discern what is the will of God—what is good and acceptable and perfect
(Romans 12:2)

Contents

Preface · ix
Acknowledgments · xi
Introduction · xiii
   Toward Holistic Transformation
   Chapter Outlines

CHAPTER 1: Models of Transformation · 1
   Four Models of Transformation

CHAPTER 2: Toward a Theory of Holistic Transformation · 11
   Three Modes of Human Existence: Heteronomy, Autonomy, and Relationality
   Three Subjects of Human Transformation: Self, Neighbor, and God
   Three Modes of Human Life: "I am no-one, I am some-one, and I am one-for-others"

CHAPTER 3: Theory of Holistic Human Transformation · 22
   Transformation through Nothingness
   Transformation Cycle
   Threefold Human Transformation

CHAPTER 4: A Transformative Reading in Hannah's Story · 38
   Marginal, Transformative Identity
   Hannah's *Han*
   The Three-Phase Transformative Process
   Conclusion

Contents

CHAPTER 5: A Transformative Reading in Psalm 13 · 48
Lament Psalms and Transformation
Overview of Lament Psalms
Overview of Psalm 13
Formal Outline of Psalm 13
Transformative Outline of Psalm 13

CHAPTER 6: A Transformative Reading in the Gospel of Mark · 58
Overview of the Gospel
Three Moments of Life in Jesus
Outlines Based on Transformation
Transformation in the Markan Community

CHAPTER 7: A Transformative Reading in Paul's Letters · 67
Paul's Transformative Experience (Gal; 1–2 Cor; Rom)
Three Moments (Modes) of Life in Paul's Transformation
Believers' Transformation in 1 Corinthians
Believers' Transformation in Romans 1–15

CHAPTER 8: Conclusion · 83

Bibliography · 89
Index · 93

Preface

IN MY BOOK *BIBLICAL Interpretation: Theory, Process, and Criteria* (2013), I affirmed the plausibility and legitimacy of the multiple interpretations because the text is read from the diverse perspectives of human life. In that book I also raised issues of the criteria for biblical interpretation because not all readings are equally helpful or valid. This book, while continuing the spirit of the previous one, focuses on aspects of human transformation when we read the Bible. Since biblical interpretation involves change in our lives, one of the crucial tasks is to read the Bible transformatively and to determine what kind of change (transformation) is desirable. This book explores those issues.

It is my conviction that the ideal self or transformation of the self is not complete without involving neighbors and God. Therefore, in this book I will examine theories of human transformation drawn from theological and philosophical traditions and explore the desirable aspects of human transformation that balances between the three kinds of transformation: a personal transformation (relation to self), a communal transformation (relation to neighbor), and a theological transformation (relation to God).

I hope this small book will invite readers to reexamine the role of the Bible in relation to the change of human life, including a change of the self and the community. I believe Paul's advice for human transformation still strikes a strong chord for our lives today: "Do not be conformed to this world, but be transformed by the renewing of your minds, so that you may discern what is the will of God—what is good and acceptable and perfect" (Rom 12:2).

Acknowledgments

WRITING ACKNOWLEDGMENTS IS A time for thanking and remembering people who were dear to me in the process of my writing. I would like to begin with the Wabash Center where I was invited to attend the 2007–8 Workshop on Teaching and Learning for Pre-Tenure Theological School Faculty. It was through the engagement with other colleagues at this place of hospitality where my book idea was nascent. I thank Paul Myhre, director of the Wabash Center, for his leadership as well as for the physical and spiritual food when we were there. I also thank all of my Wabash workshop fellows (Todd Billings, Monica Coleman, Lisa Dahill, Andrea Dickens, Elaine Heath, Tim Hessel-Robinson, Johnny Hill, Daniel Joslyn-Siemiatkoski, Melissa Kelley, Don Sik Kim, Barbara McClure, and Horace Six-Means), who took daring one-year journeys by sharing joyful and difficult things with me. Amy Oden led this remarkable workshop along with a team of excellent leaders (Rolf Jacobson, William Cahoy, and N. Lynne Westerfield). Their collective wisdom and experience ignited me with the burning desire for a deeper intellectual, spiritual journey. As a result of this workshop, I received the Wabash Fellowship that helped me to further the necessary research about human transformation in the Bible.

I also thank Daniel Patte at Vanderbilt University to whom I made a personal visit during the summer of 2008 when I conducted research on the human transformation sponsored by the Wabash Center. He laboriously read the draft with me and suggested some conceptual changes and refinement about transformation. That was a great jump-start for my constant confidence in research and writing. I also would like to give my special thanks to Larry L. Welborn at Fordham University who very much affirmed the value of this book early on and always encouraged me to go with confidence. At every Society of Biblical Literature meeting we have had privileges to talk about our mutual interests and concerns. Professor Welborn's unwavering support for me as a scholar and his enthusiastic,

Acknowledgments

sharp insight in Pauline theology has been remarkable. My special thanks also go to Jon Berquist, president of Disciples Seminary Foundation, who supported my passion and scholarly endeavors for human transformation in biblical studies. Carolyn Sharp at Yale Divinity School read the earlier version of the manuscript and helped to reshape my book. I also express my heartfelt thanks to David Bartlett at Columbia Theological Seminary who read the manuscript and supported my project. I cannot miss thanking Robert Wafawanaka, my colleague at the Samuel DeWitt Proctor School of Theology of Virginia Union University, who painstakingly read the manuscript and provided solid, helpful feedback to me. I also thank my dean, John Kinney, faculty members and staff at my school, full of the spirit of liberation and transformation.

In fact, I cannot fail to miss faith communities and people who listened to my sermons regarding human transformation. Even before writing this book, I began to preach on the story of Hannah, which I include in this book, and received very positive responses from members of the congregations and chapel services—at the assembly of the Presbytery of James, Korean immigrant churches in Nashville and Richmond, and chapel services at our school and at Union Presbyterian Seminary. It is my regret that I cannot include all of whom I owe and love so much. I thank all of these communities and people whose spirits are reflected in this book in one way or another. By the same token, I give special thanks to Roland Boer and Julie Kelso, editors of the *Journal of the Bible and Critical Theory*, who recognized the value of Hannah's transformative story and published my article in 2008 with the title of "The Story of Hannah (1 Sam 1:1—2:11) from a Perspective of *Han*: The Three-Phase Transformative Process," which became a foundational article for this current book.

Lastly, I thank my family for their full support and love, and dedicate this book to my wife Yong-Jeong and beautiful daughters, HyeRim, HyeKyung, and HyeIn. Being family means supporting each other. What matters is the love that sustains the process of tedious writing. Love you!

Introduction

HUMAN TRANSFORMATION IS AN important theme of both the Hebrew Bible and the New Testament.[1] In the Hebrew Bible, the Israelites are admonished "to turn back" to God (Hebrew *shub* in Num 14:43; Zech 1:4) from their crooked heart and their evil ways. Jesus as well as John the Baptist urges people to change their mind (*metanoeō* in Mark 1:15) for the kingdom of God. Paul exhorts people to renew their minds (*metamorphoō* in Rom 12:2) so that God's righteousness is made available to all who have faith of Jesus.[2] While the theme of transformation is abundantly present in the Bible, its content and character seems not so obvious, because the process of transformation involves many, sometimes divergent, aspects of personal, psychological, societal, and even cosmic change. Transformation may mean (1) a change of heart with a focus on one's personal relationship with God, (2) a change of heart toward particular social conditions, (3) a sense of internal peace or union with God, and (4) an apocalyptic end of the world with the arrival of a new heaven and a new earth. Those who yearn for some sort of transformation often have different visions of what that transformation might look like. While all transformation is change, not all change is desirable. So the question is what kind of transformation are we looking for? How do we know what is the best?

To illustrate the importance of human transformation in biblical studies, I share an observation about preaching. One day I was at a conference and a guest speaker was preaching about "transforming power," based on Acts 3. The summary of the sermon goes like this:

---

1. Much of this section comes from my earlier article published in *Journal of Bible and Human Transformation*. See Kim, "Rationale and Proposal."

2. Examples of transformation-related verbs include: *metamorphoo* (Rom 12:2; Matt 17:2; Mark 9:2; 2 Cor 3:18), *metaschematizoō* (2 Cor 11:13-15; Phil 3:21; 1 Cor 4:6), and *metanoeō* (Matt 3:2; Mark 1:15).

Introduction

> On a particular day when Peter and John walk up to the temple to pray, they are moved by the Spirit. They speak in the name of Jesus Christ to a lame beggar waiting at the Beautiful Gate just outside the temple. These apostles healed this lame man through transforming power that they received from God. If you receive this transforming power from God, you can do greater works like these two disciples. Jesus' name can do something bigger than you can imagine.

Sitting in a pew, I questioned to myself how God or Jesus could be different from a shaman or any deity in the ancient world. Is God simply more powerful than the other gods? Transforming power may originate from the outside source we call God, but what is missing here is talk about actual change of people involved: disciples, a lame beggar, or bystanders. In other words, I am most interested in knowing what kind of change happened to these disciples and the lame beggar when they encountered each other. Did Peter and John not change their views, renew their minds, or go through some sort of transformation in this healing scene? Likewise, what kind of transformation took place in this beggar? What kind of transformation occurred between them? What is the role of God and of Jesus in this transformation process? As this sermon shows, there are many questions we have to ask to understand transformation:

- What kind of transformation occurs, from what to what?
- How can we balance different, difficult life experiences?
- Who or what is being changed or who or what are we changing?
- What does transformation look like if it happens to self, neighbor, and God?
- What roles do these subjects (self, neighbor, God) play in transformation?
- What degree of change might be considered "transformative"?
- Are all transformative aspects equally valid in all situations?
- What is the method to get there?

As we see from the above list, the study of transformation requires interdisciplinary studies since it touches on all aspects of life. If we focus on one aspect of transformation, we can easily overlook other aspects, or in the worst case we might force others to adopt only one view of transformation. In the history of the interpretation of biblical texts, there has been a tendency of

Introduction

imposing one view over others. For instance, what is repentance in Mark 1:15 ("the time is fulfilled, and the kingdom of God has come near; repent, and believe in the good news")? For many people, "repent" is understood only as an individual confession of sins, which are not connected with a larger social world. But Jesus' message of repentance is much deeper than a personal confession of sins, because a person's life encompasses religious, political, economic, and social dimensions. Often transformation is also understood as a one-way road to a new identity or new membership in an exclusive or bounded community.

As hinted, the idea of human transformation includes a variety of aspects of change in human life, personal and/or communal. It may include change of personal views of the self, the world, and God. It can also include personal experiences that have to do with the self, the world, and God. Therefore, the aspects of change in self must be dynamic and holistic. My view of human transformation is:

- *not* a status change of one kind to another—a linear change of, for example, from a caterpillar to a butterfly—*but* a constant, dynamic, cyclical change of human attitude and sense of identity, which makes holistic transformation possible;
- *not* an overcoming or escaping of "dark" experience, mortality, or weakness *but* a making of it as part of the transformative cycle;
- *not* an individual, psychological change of "inside" only (a traditional psychotherapy) *but* an inseparable dynamic change involving self, neighbor, and God, between inside and outside of self;
- *not* the transcendence of time and space *but* the immanent transcendence in the midst of life;
- *not* like managed plants and trees *but* thriving plants and trees in a wildlife refuge that contains three moments of life, which are comparable to three modes of human attitude: 1) merciless storms making fertile soil—a mode of I am no-one; 2) the sunny breezing days good for growing plants—a mode of I am some-one; and 3) the warm spring joys of giving abundant life for visiting fish and birds for food—a mode of I am one-for-others. These three modes of human attitude can be identified in some biblical stories—especially difficult life stories such as Hannah's story.

Introduction

Toward Holistic Transformation

Holistic transformation needs new understanding about transformation itself. First, we need a conceptual change of view from a static, linear change to a dynamic, circular change that engages self, neighbor, and God. Second, transformation also means our change of view of self (and neighbor and God for that matter), not grounded in an isolated self or a fully autonomous being but based in a sense of self, which is connectional, limited, and in need of Other (including the others), and of constant change in the midst of life. Third, transformation occurs through the dynamic cycle of three moments of human life (*I am no-one, I am some-one, I am one-for-others*). Here three moments of human life can also be understood as three modes of human attitude (humbleness in nothing-like experience, confidence in self, and determination in service). Fourth, transformation means a state of balance between autonomy, heteronomy, and relationality (three modes of human existence). The goal of this transformation is not denying the self, not ignoring suffering, not suggesting a disembodied happiness, but *three-in-one* involving three moments of human life (*I am no-one, I am some-one, I am one-for-others*), and three subjects of transformation (self, neighbor, God). Finally, what I attempt to do is read biblical stories transformatively, helping readers to understand their life transformatively, as they understand this cyclic balance of human transformation in biblical stories. For example, Hannah's story can be read through three moments of human life and her engagement with self, neighbor, and God.³ Here difficult neighbors or enemies are to be part of Hannah's transformation cycle or in the process of changing her attitude ("*I am no-one, I am some-one, I am one-for-others*"); in a similar way, readers may reflect on their life parallel with Hannah's situation to find how she goes through her time of transformation.

Chapter Outlines

Chapter 1 evaluates the current status of scholarship on transformation in biblical studies. Four models of human transformation will be analyzed: Usual Western Model (*individual-autonomous*), Liberation Model (*socio-relational*), Religious Community Model (*communal-traditional*), and Religious Individual Model (*mystic, charismatic*). While each model has its

---

3. Kim, "The Story of Hannah."

Introduction

origin and context, the goal of this chapter is to understand the big picture of the current scholarship in view of transformation and to see the need for a new model of transformation (Holistic Model). Chapters 2 and 3 discuss a theory of holistic transformation in a broader context of disciplines, including political theology and psychotheology. The goal of these two chapters is to locate the topic of transformation in a wider scholarly discourse and to explore a model of holistic transformation as broadly as possible. In chapters 4–7 a few chosen texts and stories in the Bible will be read transformatively: Hannah's story (chapter 4), Psalm 13 (chapter 5), the Gospel of Mark (chapter 6), and Paul (chapter 7). Chapter 8 draws the book to a close.

CHAPTER 1

Models of Transformation

WHEN IT COMES TO the intersection of transformation and biblical studies, we cannot help but have mixed feelings. Usually, the issue of transformation is not directly dealt within biblical studies, perhaps because it is considered a topic of practical theology. Biblical scholars are not well aware of transformative implications or ramifications in their studies. Strictly speaking, however, every biblical study involves a transformative effect in one way or another: for example, transformation in the form of new knowledge or insight gained through studies or in the form of a motivational challenge in life. Whichever method we may use in biblical studies, all interpretations, including historical research, are reader-produced. If the reader is an essential coproducer of meaning along with the text, each interpretation entails a transformative effect on the reader in the present. But the problem is that some biblical scholars do not explicitly acknowledge as much of their role in interpretation as they can so as to reveal a transformative effect.

By contrast, feminist or postcolonial studies explicitly deal with transformation and challenge the androcentric, imperial interpretation of the text so as to bring a hermeneutic of liberation and justice. These days the idea of text or its meaning is much broader than times past. The more the reader engages in the text, the more he or she brings about the power of transformation. Among others, we will briefly look into some scholars who are explicitly concerned with the view of transformation. In the early 1970s Walter Wink harshly criticized the tendency of an aloof, impassionate reading of the Bible (mainly the historical-critical reading) that does not address contemporary life issues. His publications show his enthusiasm and keen analysis of both text and contemporary life. His first two books emphasize the link between biblical studies and its contemporary appropriateness to real people: *The Bible in Human Transformation* and *Transforming Bible*

A Transformative Reading of the Bible

Study.[1] His later book *The Human Being: Jesus and the Enigma of the Son of the Man*, with similar concerns about human transformation, advocates a transformative reading of the historical Jesus as an archetypal human who lived fully according to God's will.[2] This book continues the enthusiasm for human transformation in biblical studies and explores a theory of transformation with regard to other disciplines such as psychotheology and political theology.

Daniel Patte emphasizes the contextual character of biblical interpretation. His edited volume the *Global Bible Commentary* shows the power of interpretation that impacts the reader's view of text and life.[3] According to Patte, multiple interpretations are to be celebrated but not all of them are equally valid or plausible because some might be harmful or even dangerous to others in another context. Because of this kind of concern, Patte proposes three steps in the interpretation process. The first step is to recognize the reader's own issues or life contexts by which initial teaching of texts is drawn out. The second step is to compare and contrast various scholarly or ordinary readings of the given text. The third step is a deliberation state where the best interpretation is articulated as a result of critical and self-critical evaluation. Throughout the roundtable discussions members debate and discuss their interpretations. Patte makes clear that biblical interpretation has an impact on life today and, thus, that scholars are accountable for their interpretations.

Elisabeth Schüssler Fiorenza made crucial contributions to the hermeneutics of suspicion by challenging a dominant androcentric biblical scholarship that condones women's oppression and/or subordination.[4] Schüssler Fiorenza makes a distinction between the dominant male voice in the text (and in interpreters) and the oppressed female voice. Her reading is a good example of a resistant reading aimed at challenging and changing our view of a text. In this way, she has a clear purpose in studying the text because it affects our lives today. Adding to the challenge of the status quo of oppressive systems (all kinds of *kyriarchy*), this book will expand the idea of

---

1. See Wink, *The Bible in Human Transformation* and *Transforming Bible Study*.
2. Wink, *The Human Being*.
3. Patte, ed., *Global Bible Commentary*. Patte's recognition of diverse aspects of world Christianity led him to editing *Cambridge Dictionary of Christianity*. See also *Discipleship, Ethics of Biblical Interpretation*.
4. Schüssler Fiorenza, *Rights at Risk*; *The Power of the Word*; and *Rhetoric and Ethic*.

transformation to cover all aspects of life that involve self, neighbor (or enemy), and God.

Besides these biblical scholars, Eric Santner needs to be mentioned. In his book *On the Psychotheology of Everyday Life: Reflections on Freud and Rosenzweig*, Santner claims that human transformation is possible in the midst of life—even in the deepest valleys of "dark" moments in life.[5] Having Sigmund Freud and Franz Rosenzweig (Freud's contemporary and a Jewish theologian) in conversation, he argues that Freudian unconsciousness or difficult moments of life can be transformative when looked through Rosenzweig's theological lens; such a dark moment becomes a moment of divine revelation. Santner echoes my understanding of transformation based on the "I am no-one" experience, which is one of the three moments of human life: "I am no-one, I am some-one, I am one-for-others." Similarly, in the study of political theology Slavoj Žižek, Eric Santner, and Kenneth Reinhard also share my understanding of neighbor or enemy, which has a role in human transformation.[6]

Four Models of Transformation

Biblical studies are ideological in the sense that "ideology represents the imaginary relationship of individuals to their real conditions of life."[7] Likewise, our studies on transformation are also ideological in the way that transformation is approached differently depending on an interpreter's ideology. Thus, it is not easy to analyze the variety of understanding about transformation informed by ideology. However, one of the best ways to analyze various models of human transformation in biblical studies is to examine *three modes of human existence*, namely, autonomy (a mode of rule by self), relationality (a mode of rule by community), and heteronomy (rule by Other), because these modes reflect scholars' view of an ideal transformation in terms of individual life (autonomy), communal life (relationality), and religious experience (heteronomy). As these three modes of human existence imply, human life is complex and vibrant. An appropriate question concenring transformation might be: "What am I here to live in this world and in relation to others and God?" Some emphasize autonomy as a main mode of human existence, and thus transformation is understood

---

5. Santner, *On the Psychotheology of Everyday Life*.
6. Žižek, Santner, and Reinhard, *The Neighbor*.
7. Althusser, "Ideology and Ideology State Apparatuses," 162.

as autonomous life. Likewise, different philosophical schools, or various biblical, theological traditions emphasize certain mode(s) against other modes. Depending on their emphasis on different modes of human existence, the following five models emerge in biblical studies (the last model is mine):

- Usual Western Model (*individual-autonomous* transformation)
- Liberation Model (*socio-relational* transformation)
- Religious Community Model (*traditional-communal* transformation)
- Religious Individual Model (*mystic, charismatic* transformation)
- Holistic Model (*three-in-one transformation*)

All these models have certain values or merits with certain emphasis of transformation. But one model cannot cover all aspects of human transformation. In some cases, a certain model might not be helpful for others in another situation. Though each model is plausible or valid in certain contexts, it should not be applied to all people in all contexts.

Usual Western Model (Individual-Autonomous Transformation)

With the shorthand of "A" standing for autonomy, "H" for heteronomy, and "R" for relationality, the Usual Western Model can be designated "A-H-R" or "A-R-H," in the sense that autonomy is a decisive force or mode of human existence and informs the other two modes. In this model the implicit agenda of human transformation has to do with the recovery of individuality—one can decide one's own life (autonomy). This autonomy-driven model has its root in the Enlightenment and emerged as a countercultural movement to the authoritarianism or theocracy. This recovery of autonomy is a great achievement in human history. In a way, modernity continues as its spirit throws the unending suspicion to any form of a destructive abusive authoritarian rule whether in religious discourse or in political global arena.

In biblical studies this awareness of critical autonomy leads to the historical-critical mindset. The historically conscious methods such as source criticism or redaction criticism help readers be critically aware of history of ancient people, that is, these methods reveal sheer information or knowledge about ancient people, communities, and societies. So the great value of this model is that nobody can twist meanings of a text, betraying

Models of Transformation

historical rootedness. This, however, does not mean that this model guarantees an objective meaning of text.

This Western model also has a transformative effect on the interpreter or the reader who gains new understanding (knowledge or information) about history (and text) and its applicability to the present life. There is a two-step meaning structure in this model: what it meant then and what it means now. The interpreter or the reader is to do or act on the basis of new knowledge or information gained from historical studies.

In their commentary on Matthew, Davies and Allison read Matthew 28:16–20 with a focus on "A-H-R" sequence of transformation.[8] Discipleship involves what Jesus' disciples already know (correct knowledge or understanding) and going out to encourage others to follow this knowledge of theirs. An individual Christian is equipped by correct knowledge (autonomy), is confirmed or supported by the presence of the Lord (heteronomy), and affects other non-Christian people (relationality).

In terms of an ethical view, this sub-model (A-H-R) belongs to the "deontological" view of moral life. As Jesus commands, disciples become who they are (having truth and knowing the gospel). Jesus transfers his power or authority to them. Individual Christians receive the same authority to preach the gospel to others. They are self-sufficient in the way that they do not depend on others, other traditions, or experiences of others. In this sub-model, transformation is understood as having the sense of new life and new identity. Certainly this model has effect on people who are struggling with their own identity. However, this model could have negative connotations: for example, "I know but you do not know; so you should know what I know." Historically this model has been employed with negative consequences for other peoples and cultures.[9]

Daniel Patte's reading of Matthew 28:16–20 is an "A-R-H" sequence of transformation, with a notion of autonomy that is very different from Davies and Allison.[10] For Patte, autonomy is informed and understood by the theology of *the least* (as seen in the last judgment episode and Jesus' cross). That is, who I am as an autonomous Christian is to be enlightened by the face of Jesus seen in the least fortunate in society. This emphasis on "the cross-informed" autonomy concerns the existence of others, the life of a community, and society as a whole (the mode of relationality). But this

---

8. Davies and Allison, *Matthew*, 676–89.
9. Hutchison, *Errand to the World*.
10. Patte, "Reading Matthew 28:16–20 with Others."

autonomy working toward relationality is to be governed by the rule of God (heteronomy). In this way, Patte complements weaknesses of autonomy by critical awareness of relationality and the corrective force of God's rule. In terms of an ethical view, this sub-model presents the perfectionist view of moral life in the way that Jesus' cross-based experience and ministry is the point of what believers should follow. The vision of a just community based on Jesus' life and death is none other than living for the least or the oppressed.

In summary, the Usual Western Model places autonomy at the top. While autonomy is important in human transformation, this model may miss the critical awareness of subjectivity (intersubjectivity) that involves other modes of human life (heteronomy and relationality).

Liberation Model (Social-Relational Transformation)

In the Liberation Model, relationality is the primary mode of human existence, and the two other modes (autonomy, heteronomy) follow. We can designate it either "R-A-H" or "R-H-A," in the sense that relationality is the primary, operative mode in human life: individual relationships within a community, relations between communities, relations between individuals and a community, or between individuals and society. Aiming at social justice and human freedom, this model challenges various oppressive human ideologies or social evils. Liberation theologians advocate for economic justice (and therefore liberation from the shackles of economic injustice), feminist theologians emphasize equality of gender (so liberation from the gendered oppression), and postcolonial theorists advocate for equality of power and structure (liberation from the imperial oppressions).[11]

In this model, transformation means social change that brings equality, freedom, and justice to people. If life conditions of the world

---

11. Musa Dube's interpretation of Matthew 28 is a case in point. From a postcolonial perspective she problematizes all kinds of oppressive readings. Matthew 28:16–20 becomes the weapon of dominance and control by Western missionaries; disciples are commissioned to go *anywhere*, disavowing geographical borders. Both an imperial/colonial text and readings of imperial/colonial readers are equally challenged. The most urgent issue is liberation from the ideologies of oppression and suppression of others. The affirmation here is that if this problem of dominance is remedied, personal human dignity or justice will be recovered. Such a life of recovery is the rule of God (heteronomy). So implicitly her reading is a model of R-A-H even though Musa does not elaborate on the relationships between three modes.

Models of Transformation

(relationality) are set right, there will be a good life with a sense of dignity and autonomy. Otherwise, this model does not discuss explicitly the causal relationships between three modes of human existence. In summary, the Liberation Model, with its varieties of interpretation, has merits of advancing human welfare and justice by challenging various ideologies of dominance or control.[12]

Religious Community Model (Traditional-Communal Transformation)

The Religious Community Model begins with heteronomy as a primary mode—a special "religious experience" bestowed to a community. We can designate model "H-R-A."[13] The modes of human existence move from

---

12. There are actually different interpretations of Matthew 28 within the "R-A-H" model. Like Dube, George Soares-Prabhu also has concerns about Western missionary activities, but for him the real problem is not so much the oppressive text as a lack of true discipleship. Namely, disciples or missionaries are not well informed or renewed in light of welfare for all people. Soares-Prabhu questions autonomy in light of relationality (community and the larger world), asking what discipleship has to do with the other, and what kind of disciples they should be (disposition). Autonomy needs to be self-critiqued or renewed in view of the most important mission, which is welfare for all people. In this regard, Soares-Prabhu's concept of autonomy is not Western; rather, it is close to "inter-subjectivity." Examining a contemporary social world (relationality) in terms of world community and world well-being, he deepens the sense of autonomy (individual disciples or Christians) informed by relationality. As a result of this kind of discipleship, the rule of God is established (heteronomy). On the other hand, Elaine Wainwright's reading of Matthew 28 is "R-H-A." As a feminist biblical critic, she challenges the androcentric interpretation of Matthew 28 where Jesus commissions only male disciples. Being concerned about gendered understanding of discipleship, Wainwright elevates women's faith as a model of discipleship; women are indeed first witnesses to Jesus' resurrection. They tell male disciples about their experience of the risen Lord. Then male disciples are supposed to recover from their guilt or failure in the past. They are commissioned only after this humbling process of recovery from the past. In terms of transformation, Wainwright begins with the mode of relationality because of women's oppression or gender inequality in a community. Women encountering Jesus at the tomb is the mode of heteronomy—women's total surprise in the midst of hopelessness. This wondrous experience of heteronomy is a basis of who they are (autonomy). They realize they are equal disciples who witnessed and witnessed to Jesus' death and resurrection. See Dube, "'Go Therefore,'" 224–45; Wainwright, *Shall We Look*, 114; Soares-Prabhu, "Two Mission Commands," 319–39.

13. Raymond Brown and Daniel Harrington follow an "H-R-A" model in their interpretation of Matt 28:16–20. For them Jesus Messiah represents a new Israel and forms a new church (a new messianic community) in the new epoch. The Gospel of Matthew

7

heteronomy (in the form of a special revelation or experience) to relationality (their view of the world as such) to autonomy (very weak sense of individuality in this case).[14] Roman Catholic tradition and Greek Orthodox tradition also have a tendency toward this model of transformation. That is, the heteronomy is established through apostolic succession or church interpretation of scriptures. This mode of heteronomy legitimates church hierarchy or structure. Even the whole world is viewed through this order. The world belongs to the church. The dictum of "no salvation outside of the church" can be understood from this light. Individual members are to follow this tradition and leadership because it comes from divine origin (heteronomy). Unlike from Usual Western Model, the mode of autonomy does not operate strongly in this model.

Benefits of this model are such that members of a community have a strong sense of identity and strong community leadership supported by divine origin. However, the weakness of this model comes from the opposite side of the Western Individual Model. Heteronomy as the primary mode of human existence dictates the other two modes, determining their identity or behavior, including members' relation to God and the world. There is little room for a challenge or critique to the tradition or to the role of heteronomy, when in fact, heteronomy is not always a one-way road; it involves diverse aspects of life, including the role of outsiders. Similarly, there is not much of a role for autonomous individuals who have to engage others in other cultures.

---

is the only gospel that explicitly mentions church (*ekklesia*). Jesus declares that he will build *his* church on the rock (*petros* in Greek from which the name Peter is derived). Peter is considered the first foundation of the church. *Ekklesia* is possible through a new revelation of Jesus (Jesus' revelation or Christology is a heteronomy experience) and is founded upon Peter. In other words, Christology is the foundation of a new community (ecclesiology). See Kingsbury, *Matthew*, 1–39.

14. The Qumran community in the first century CE is a good example of this model. This community has its own charismatic leaders, community rules, and authoritative books and commentaries. The Qumran community teaches that an imminent end of the world comes through a cosmic struggle between light and darkness. For this community, transformation begins with a radical break from the corrupt leadership of the Jerusalem Temple, and will be completed at the last day when they enter the new world. In fact, this community's vision for salvation or transformation is very different from others such as the Pharisees, who emphasize renewal of people through the diligent study and practice of the law in their daily lives. In strict community life, members of the community believe that salvation and transformation are exclusive to them.

Models of Transformation

Religious Individual Model (Mystic, Charismatic Transformation)

The Religious Individual Model differs from the Religious Community Model in the way that it focuses on charismatic, mystic *individual leaders* who exercise special revelations received from God.

Based on this kind of special heteronomy, these indivduals serve as powerful leaders in the community. Members of the community are to follow this heteronomy and rule of their leaders. That is the basis of who they are (sense of self-identity as autonomy). The community is the sum of these individuals. Thus it is an "H-A-R" sequence model: the special religious experience-driven heteronomy (charismatic leaders) informs individual members (autonomy) about their thought and behavior. The community (relationality) is a result of this sequence of H-A. The critical role of community is deemphasized as compared to the Religious Community Model because individual leaders have authority over the community. This is the weakness of the model. The members of a community are gathered to hear special charismatic leaders who teach in the name of God (heteronomy). Likewise, the conception of community is narrow and does not include others outside of it. There is no critical role of individuals either. This model lacks a critical democratic spirit or a critical awareness of individual human capacity. Taken all together, there is no system of checks and balances between charismatic leaders and the community, and between these individual leaders and their claim of heteronomy. As we see in the Usual Western Model, the role of human agency or the role of critical autonomy is very important.

Despite many weaknesses, if understood and practiced well, this model may complement the other models. For instance, if any charismatic leaders are well informed by a healthy theology (heteronomy), the conditions of the social political world (relationality), and intersubjectivity of the self, which includes other stories, this model would work well too. But in reality, it is hardly the case. Rather, what is emphasized is individual charismatic leadership, strong boundaries, and ignorance of others and of a wider community.

Holistic Model (Three-in-One Transformation)

Thus far we have examined four models of transformation in biblical studies, using an analytical tool of three modes of human existence. Often one mode of human existence is emphasized at the sacrifice of others and ignores other important aspects of human transformation. Even though we cannot cover all complexities of biblical interpretation and its relation to ways of transformation, what is analyzed here can be a heuristic key to tell us what is lacking there: a lack of holism in human transformation that will be discussed and explored in the next two chapters. This holistic model looks for a balance in human transformation in both personal and public life. It strives for a balance between the three modes of human existence (autonomy, heteronomy, and relationality), between three moments of human life (*I am no-one, I am some-one, I am one-for-others*), and between three subjects of human transformation (self, neighbor, God). While all forms of transformation are change, not all change is equally valid or desirable. How do we know which is the best? This question is the topic of the next two chapters.

CHAPTER 2

Toward a Theory of Holistic Transformation

In the previous chapter we explored four models of transformation in biblical studies. In this chapter a theory of holistic transformation will be explored with consideration of fields such as philosophy, political theology, and psychotheology. To begin, the following list of questions raised in the introduction will be helpful to review since it covers a variety of issues concerning holistic transformation:

- What kind of transformation occurs, from what to what?
- How can we balance different, difficult life experiences?
- Who or what is being changed, or who or what are we changing?
- What does transformation look like if it happens to self, neighbor, and God?
- What roles do these subjects (self, neighbor, God) play in transformation?
- What degree of change might be considered "transformative"?
- Are all transformative aspects equally valid in all situations?
- What is the method to get there?

In analyzing various scholarly traditions of transformation, we will pay attention to how each tradition understands transformation. What are some assumptions of each tradition? The analytical tools for this task are (1) three modes of human existence, (2) three subjects of human transformation, and (3) three moments (modes) of human life. The three modes of human existence include autonomy, heteronomy, and relationality. The three subjects of human transformation include self, neighbor, and God. Three modes of human life include *I am no-one, I am some-one, and I am one-for-others*. In the following, I will explain how each of these tools is understood and used in this book.

Three Modes of Human Existence: Autonomy, Heteronomy, and Relationality

In intellectual traditions, more or less, one mode of human existence is emphasized over against the other. While autonomy-driven human transformation emphasizes the role of subjectivity (individuals as moral subjects) and clear boundaries between good and bad, relationality-driven human transformation underscores the role of community and justice in society. In heteronomy-driven human transformation, the role of "others" (or Other) is highly emphasized. Let us look at these traditions one by one.

First, regarding the autonomy-driven human transformation we can begin with Kant because he is a sort of bridge philosopher who both inherits and critiques Western Enlightenment tradition. For Kant autonomy is limited because human minds can reach only *phenomena*, not *noumena*. However, a human mind is capable enough to maintain a good moral world if it knows duties. An individual self (person) can be a moral agent, who can change society, making moral good. Kant continues the Enlightenment tradition with an emphasis on autonomy-driven human transformation. Otherwise, Kant does not elaborate on relationality or community perhaps because community or society is considered the sum of individuals. Likewise, there is no sense of intersubjectivity for him. In a way, his human mind reaches the entire world without actually traveling it (he actually never traveled outside his home country). Heteronomy is denied simply because it cannot be known. As a result, Kant misses diverse aspects of human life in the world, much less the role of others.

Second, regarding relationality-driven human transformation we can begin with Nietzsche, who radically challenges modernity by challenging the ineffectiveness of autonomy or heteronomy to bring justice or diversity to human life. For Nietzsche, the gravest problem is that the diversity of life based in justice was sacrificed in the name of God (heteronomy). In this context he declares "the death of God"—the God that legitimates interests of powerful elites at the sacrifice of the marginalized. Nietzsche's declaration is not an ontological claim of God's death as such, but an ideological counterclaim that such an all-powerful God who cannot do justice must be dead. His rhetoric is a challenge to those who use God as an ultimate

Toward a Theory of Holistic Transformation

power while suppressing the truth. In this way, Nietzsche begins to break the strong walls of the Enlightenment autonomy and an ideal of unity.[1]

It is Jacques Derrida who gave a decisive blow to the idea of autonomy in modern culture by deconstructing our notion of text and readers.[2] His "deconstruction" in literary studies addresses the issue of relationality—how to live with others in different contexts. His notion of relationality is well expressed by his oxymoronic phrase, "relationless relation," which is a negative expression that emphasizes a radical-diversity-driven community.[3] That is to say, if there is any relation possible in the world, it should be relationless in the sense that relation is not to be constructed unilaterally. This phrase implies that there should be an ongoing, difficult dialogue between different parties or persons, not attempting to forge an easy relation based on his or her own position. In this attempt of dialogue, the previous meaning or significance can be deconstructed and reconstructed time and again. For Derrida, transformation is possible when there is true diversity in human life along with justice. So he challenges logocentrism because it denies differences or diversity in human life.[4]

Third, regarding heteronomy-driven human transformation we can begin with Freud, the psychoanalyst who draws our attention to the "unconsciousness" in our human psyche as "others," which is another form of heteronomy. This uncanny presence called the unconsciousness is dormant in us and thereby rules us. In a pre-Kantian version of the view of this kind of strangeness, everything is to be explained between good and bad,

---

1. Levinas and Ricoeur continue the spirit of Nietzsche, and complement the idea of autonomy by incorporating the role of others: "The face of the Other" (Levinas) and "narrative identity or inter-subjectivity" (Ricoeur). See Levinas, *Totality and Infinity*; Ricoeur, *Time and Narrative*, vol. 3.

2. Derrida, "Différance." See also his interview, "Villanova Roundtable."

3. Derrida, "Villanova Roundtable," 13.

4. Postcolonial critics also emphasize "relationality" to underscore the problem of domination and control by the colonial powers. The view of transformation is to live with justice and dignity in society. Likewise, this mode of relationality is very much emphasized in *minjung* theology (a kind of liberation theology) when Korea underwent political turmoil in 1970s-80s without human rights. *Minjung* is a term for the grassroots, those who are the majority of powerless people. Jesus is a representative of the *minjung* who advocates liberation of human beings. The theory of minjung theology bases the social message of the kingdom of God, for which Jesus, as a liberator and social prophet, not as an otherworldly messiah, sides with *minjung*. A new world of full humanity is envisioned. Otherwise, *minjung* theology does not explicitly discuss the human self (autonomy) or heteronomy, or the relational aspects of the three modes combined. See Kim and Kim, eds., *Reading Minjung Theology*.

A Transformative Reading of the Bible

between light and darkness, between normal and abnormal, and between overcoming and overcame, which means there is no unknowable area or thing in the human life and psyche. But Freud acknowledges the existence of the unknowable area in our psyche. He is awakened to this existence of something more than we normally think we are. This unknowable, strange power inside human psyche is a mode of heteronomy at which, according to Franz Rosenzweig, divine intervention takes place. As Eric Santner points out, when we read Freud's unconsciousness (heteronomy) through Rosenzweig's theological eyes, Freud's heteronomy is significant because it is the mode at which divinity is encountered.[5] Rosenzweig theologizes the meaning of event (a moment of darkness, a meaningless, difficult thing) and sees the possibility of transformation in it. In this moment of nothingness, our life has a hopeful, changeable moment even when we are not in control of it.

In each of these traditions there are pros and cons. What remains to be seen in an ideal human transformation is how to articulate the relations between these three modes of human existence to which we will return in the next chapter.

Three Subjects of Human Transformation: Self, Neighbor, and God

In this section we take a look at another side of transformation involving political theology in which the interrelatedness of self, neighbor, and God are important. The issue here is how we can explore the interrelatedness between these three. Let us begin with Freud's understanding of this topic. Freud has a strong desire to protect the self, which is almost a holy entity. Given his witness of the indignities perpetrated under the guise of nationalism and ideologies during the First World War, Freud's preoccupation with the self is understandable. In this context, Freud thinks that evil is evil so there is no room for loving the evil or enemy. The love of enemy is simply unacceptable, unjust, or even unethical to that person who was victimized. What is hateful is hateful and must be hated. In other words, there should be a clear boundary between good and bad; otherwise the self will be suffocated and lost. Freud, thus, throws suspicion to the biblical injunction "love one's neighbor as oneself" (Lev 19:18 and NT), as he states:[6]

5. Santner, *On the Psychotheology of Everyday Life*, 77, 90–92.
6. Freud, *Civilization and Its Discontents*, 66.

> What would we do it? What good will it do to us? But, above all, how shall we achieve it? How can it be possible? My love is something valuable to me which I ought not to throw away without reflection. It imposes duties on me for whose fulfillment I must be ready to make sacrifices. If I love someone, he must deserve it in some way.... He deserves it if he is so like me in important ways that I can love myself in him; and he deserves it if he is so much more perfect than myself that I can love my ideal of my own self in him.

Freud does not engage difficult neighbors (enemies). The self is to be protected from the negative effects of the enemy. For Freud, one of the basic rules of psychotherapy is to discharge "too much" of life's burdens because humans cannot bear much beyond their capacity. For example, if pain or suffering caused by an enemy creates an unnecessary psychological lump, this must be released just like the removal of the cancer cells in our bodies. Even though Freud recognizes the mode of heteronomy in the form of dormant unconsciousness, his notion of self ironically does not engage the difficult neighbor. Freud sees a self reaching the deepest depths of the human psyche, seeing deeper than Kant's universe, but he himself does not engage in this complex self. The irony is that his insight has a political and theological implications for human transformation (because strangeness can be a moment of life-changing experience), and yet he does not engage difficult neighbors or enemies in any politico-theological sense.

Critiquing this kind of Freudian thinking, Kenneth Reinhard suggests that our engaging of difficult neighbors will keep the political process alive and healthy. Jacques Derrida similarly notes that a country without enemy is more dangerous than the country surrounded by enemies.[7] There is a role for enemies or "others" or "strangers" in political life. Otherwise, it will be another form of dictatorship.

However, the boundary between friend and enemy is not always clear-cut and collapses at times. Žižek points out, for example, that Israeli soldiers who refuse the command to kill Palestinian soldiers, their enemies, violate the boundary between enemy and friend at the risk of their own security and identity. Giorgio Agamben also points out the problem of a clear boundary between friend and enemy, or between the worthy and unworthy, when he discusses *homo sacer* (referred to as a slave who is legally unholy to be sacrificed and so can be killed without guilt). Alain Badiou

---

7. Derrida, *The Politics of Friendship*, 83.

A Transformative Reading of the Bible

also challenges an artificial boundary between friend and enemy by emphasizing the role of "love," which "fractures the imaginary unity."[8]

But according to Reinhard, this issue of the boundary between friend and enemy can be resolved when *three loves* (of self, of neighbor, and of God) are placed in a critical dialogue. Namely, when these *three loves* intersect each other, the boundary melts or stays healthy with necessary tensions because "the relationship between any two terms requires the third: the subject loves the neighbor only by means of the love of God, and loves God only by means of the love of the neighbor."[9] What he means by these three loves is well stated in the following:

> Love of myself is imaginary, the spectacular reflection on myself that constitutes the narcissistic ego in the mirror stage; and love of the neighbor is real, insofar as the neighbor harbors the strange kernel of enjoyment Freud and Lacan call the Thing. However, this twoness cannot be reached directly and does not subsist on its own, Lacan argues, except by passing by way of the third love, never superseded, the love of God, which is the model of symbolic love, the love of the father that sustains the symbolic order. Hence, love of the neighbor includes within it the love of God, and together they constitute the Borromean knot of political theology. The subject loves the neighbor only by means of the love of God, and loves God only by means of the love of the neighbor.[10]

In summary, the three subjects of transformation (self, neighbor, and God) can work together in political theology. These three should have "inconvenient" tense relations so that healthy transformation might take place. This insight of political theology will inform our transformative reading of the Bible since the Bible is also a political theological story.

Three Modes of Human Life: I am No-One, I Am Some-One, and I Am One-For-Others

Lastly, in this section we will take a look at another dimension of human transformation that involves various moments or modes of human life: *I am no-one, I am some-one, and I am one-for-others*. *I am no-one* stands for a moment of life in which one can feel nobody or nothing. *I am some-one*

---

8. Reinhard, "Toward a Political Theology of the Neighbor," 68.
9. Ibid., 72–73.
10. Ibid., 71–72.

Toward a Theory of Holistic Transformation

stands for a moment of life in which one can feel somebody special. *I am one-for-others* stands for a moment of life in which one can feel committed to service, willing to become anybody for others. We can also apply these three moments of life to attitudinal modes: "humility before God (and others)," confidence in one's identity, and willingness to engage others. The problem in our lives is that we tend to separate these three modes. For instance, if any one thinks he or she is great (*I am some-one*) without having a mode of humility (*I am no-one*), that person would be a naïve thinker who does not touch on real life change in the world. If any one thinks he or she can serve others (*I am one-for-others*) without having a sense of *I am no-one*, that service could be manipulative or dangerous.

In some branches of traditional theology if anyone goes through a difficult life (suffering or pain), there must be something wrong with him or her, because every act has a consequence in terms of "a system of reward and punishment" (well preserved in the so-called Deuteronomic school: Deuteronomy to 1–2 Kings).[11] Likewise, human mortality, illness, vulnerability, or any other forms of weakness are related to the result of human sin or God's punishment. In that theology the world is viewed as a transitory place, and the true home is never here. The garden of Eden, the perfect world, is lost; so the ultimate hope is to recover it where there are tears or death no more. Accordingly, transformation means a move from *I am no-one* (an old sinful status) to *I am some-one* (a new humanity in Christ). As a result, he or she works for others (*I am one-for-others*). This view of transformation is linear, otherworldly, and duty-ethics (a kind of ethics of "indicative-imperative"—"become what you are"). Otherwise, there is no

---

11. Job's suffering is often read from this perspective of reward and punishment, but the whole story does not support such a view. There is no reason found in the book why Job suffers. We only know from this story that we are not completely crushed in the midst of total darkness as long as we do not give up our faith in God. If Job's story is not about a test of faith, it can be read transformatively in the way that his difficult life experience is processed through a long time of personal struggle with his family, friends, enemies, and God. The long middle section of Job (chapters 3–41) is added in the process of story development to reflect the importance of dialogue or engagement of difficult experience. The original tradition or story seemed simple, as a story of test and faith (prologue) in Job 1–2, and a story of "order and freedom in felicity" (epilogue) in Job 42:7–17. Through Job's story, we learn how Job goes through his *I am no-one*, and how he is not given in to that status. But through it, he encounters in a new way God, who speaks in the midst of chaos, and yet spares answering why he suffers, other than reminding him of his human mortality and the need of faith in the midst of nothingness. See Janzen, *Job*, 31–33, 261–69.

A Transformative Reading of the Bible

positive role of human weakness, sickness, or any form of dark experience in this world.

L. Anne Jervis's interpretation of sin and suffering is an example of this linear model. In her book *At the Heart of the Gospel: Suffering in the Earliest Christian Message*, Jervis follows a classical view of sin and suffering in that the ultimate hope is to go to the final kingdom of God at consummation.[12] Time here on earth is a state of uncertainty or punishment. Sin is the name for evil and the cause of every suffering, including human mortality. Like Augustine's concept of original sin, according to which humanity is born with sinful contamination, Jervis makes haste to point out sin's problem in Paul's theology without seriously considering human problems in Paul's letters. So if sin's power is destroyed by Christ's power, all problems, including suffering, will be remedied. That will happen in the end. Until then, there will still be suffering in the world.

But the real problem for Paul is not sin's problem or the law's problem but the human problem of unfaithfulness that brings suffering and chaos to the world. This means that suffering of the world can be addressed and partially resolved by human participation in Christ's death, which means setting minds on "the things of the Spirit" rather than on "the things of the flesh" (Rom 8:5–6), or further, "putting to death the deeds of the body" (Rom 8:13). When this happens sin's power is undone even though we do not know from where it comes. Though sin is powerful, it loses its power when believers are dead to it (by putting to death the deeds of the body). Then sin does not seize an opportunity of the law to exercise its power over the human mind. The point is human transformation is possible through human participation with Christ and that there must be a role for suffering in the world even though unwanted. Human participation with Christ means to participate in his suffering or grief. Jesus' death does not remove sin or suffering but urges believers to participate in his death to transform the world and self. For this job, Paul says, "I have been crucified with Christ" (Gal 2:19). Here Christ's death or suffering is a result of his obedience to the love of God. Similarly, the believer's job is to have Christ's faithfulness.

For Paul pain or suffering in the world is not merely something to be escaped or to be removed by Christ's death once and for all. Rather it challenges and engages believers in a new way so that the suffering of the world can be transformed with mutual crucifixion: "May I never boast of anything except the cross of our Lord Jesus Christ, by which the world has

---

12. Jervis, *At the Heart of the Gospel*.

been crucified to me, and I to the world" (Gal 6: 14). The deathlike life situation faced by slaves or the low class members of the Pauline communities cannot be ignored because of the future salvation in the kingdom of God; rather, it will empower those overpowered to experience the power of the cross in their daily lives, as Welborn rightly observes:

> The message that the Christ had shared the fate of a piece of human garbage, one of those whom life had demolished, and who had touched bottom—this message was a power capable of rescuing those who trusted in it from despair over the nothingness of their lives (1 Cor. 1:18b, 21b, 24), so that, even if they lived in the shadow of the cross and died a bit every day, and even if the cross should be their tomb, as it was of their fathers and grandfathers, its power over them was broken and undone, so that they could live-on with value and meaning and love and hope, because the one who had died in this contemptible way was the anointed one of God.[13]

What matters in human transformation is a "die and live" theology of Paul. In this sense, philosopher Walter Benjamin is right when he emphasizes dying and living-on together in human transformation.[14] In contrast to Alain Badiou, who emphasizes resurrection as a decisive moment of breaking away from a death-situation, Benjamin sees the moment of difficult life as a shock or fragmentary life experience through which one can live transformatively.[15] For Paul the cross of Jesus and the suffering of the people and the world cannot be separate in the sense that "Jesus died instead of me" (Jesus' death as a substitution); rather, Paul writes: "one died for all, and therefore all died. And on behalf of all he died, so that those who live might live no longer for themselves, but for the one who for their sake died and was raised" (2 Cor 5:14–15).[16] So transformation takes place through both "dying and living-on" together:

> But we have this treasure in earthen vessels, so that it may be clear that this extraordinary power belongs to God and does not come

---

13. Welborn, "Extraction from the Mortal Site," 295–314. Welborn discusses the significance of Paul's theology of death rooted in the people of the Greco-Roman world, especially in the low class and slaves. He argues that the cross of Christ Jesus has transformative, redemptive effect on these people who are crucified.

14. Benjamin, "The Task of the Translator," 253–63; Chowdhury, "Memory, Modernity, Repetition," 28–29.

15. Badiou, *Saint Paul*, 70–73. See Benjamin, "The Task of the Translator," 253–63.

16. See the comments on this text by Bultmann, *Der zweite Brief an die Korinther*.

A Transformative Reading of the Bible

> from us. We are afflicted in every way, but not crushed; perplexed, but not driven to despair; persecuted, but not forsaken; struck down, but not destroyed; always carrying about in our body the mortification [*nekrosis*] of Jesus, in order that the life of Jesus may be manifest in our body. For constantly we the living are being handed over into death on account of Jesus, so that the life of Jesus may be manifest in our mortal flesh. (2 Cor 4:7–11)

Interestingly, Stoics generally avoid talking about pain or suffering, especially in the context of slaves' death because it is too cruel to talk about, or simply they close their eyes and mind to keep forgetting it. In a sense, they do not seem to know how to handle this overbearing grief or human tragedy. Stoics actually always provide alternative virtues or emotions: joy (*chara*) in place of pleasure (*hedone*), volition (*boulesis*) in place of desire (*epithumia*), and caution (*eulabeia*) in place of fear (*phobos*).[17] But they do not find an alternative to pain (*lype*).[18] This is because, in the Stoics' thought, there is no role of pain in human transformation other than considering it taboo or burying it forever in the human mind.

In Paul's theology, however, suffering or pain has an essential role to play in human transformation, as we see in 2 Cor 7:9: "Now I rejoice, not because you were grieved, but because your grief led to repentance; for you felt *a godly grief*, so that you were not harmed in any way by us." Not just any grief but the grief leading to transformation is crucial in Paul's theology in the way that Christ's cross is an ultimate expression of a godly grief in which Jesus died and lived for God and God's people. From the perspective of godly pain, this pain cannot pass by simply because it is too cruel or difficult. Rather, by identifying with Christ's death (his grief), the believer joins in his suffering (a mode of *I am no-one*)—a moment of pain and suffering because of the love of God. For Paul, this mode of *I am no-one* includes not only persecutions due to his mission work but his personal weaknesses of character or physical conditions. So he always confesses that he is *nothing* or *I am no-one* (the least of the apostles) and that the way he is now (*I am some-one*) is because of God's grace (1 Cor 15:9–10), which empowers him to serve people (*I am one-for-others*). Moreover, Paul affirms these three modes of life or three modes of attitude in Phil 3:7–9: "Yet whatever gains I had, these I have come to regard as loss because of Christ. More than that, I regard everything as loss because of the surpassing value of knowing

---

17. Pereboom "Stoic Psychotherapy," 592–625.
18. Welborn, "Paul and Pain," 547–70.

Christ Jesus my Lord. For his sake I have *suffered the loss of all things* [*I am no-one*], and I regard them as rubbish, in order that I may *gain Christ and be found in him* [*I am some-one*], not having a righteousness of my own that comes from the law, but one that comes *through faith of Christ* [*I am one-for-others*], the righteousness from God based on faith." Paul does not say the law is impossible for righteousness because it is law; rather, for Paul, the problem is when the law is not based on faith. But Christ fulfills the law (Rom 10:4) through his faith, which is to follow God's law, or the law of God, which mandates love and justice for all people, as opposed to the law of sin. As we see here briefly, Paul's understanding of transformation is not based on departure from one status to another but through living faithfully through pain and suffering, which involves three modes of human attitude or human life in balance.

Let me summarize what we have discussed so far before we move on to explore a theory of holistic transformation. Against the traditional view of *I am no-one* (suffering or pain) or against the linear view of change (a change from *I am no-one* to *I am some-one* to *I am one-for-others*), I suggest that nothing-like life is considered as an essential part of life, which can spur the process of transformation. Recently, some feminist theologians have embraced the limits and weaknesses of humanity as part of life and have come to appreciate the possibilities of transformation because of them.[19] Rather than seeking fantasies like a mirage in the desert, or seeking something new beyond this world, we can enter the process of transformation right here in the middle of life—amidst a variety of life experiences. The question is: how can we incorporate and articulate all different moments of life, namely three moments of life in our exploration of transformation? This question will be addressed in the next chapter.

---

19. Welch, *A Feminist Ethic of Risk*.

CHAPTER 3

Theory of a Holistic Human Transformation

USING THE PRECEDING DISCUSSIONS about holistic transformation, we will now explore a theory of holistic transformation.[1] In so doing, we have to ask the following questions:

- Why are there three moments (modes) in our lives?
- How is a balance between three moments of life achieved?
- How are these three modes of human existence (autonomy, heteronomy, and relationality) related with each other in an ideal human transformation?
- How are the three subjects of human transformation (self, neighbor, and God) related to the three moments (modes) of life?

Transformation through "Nothingness"

A psalmist walked in the valley of death and faced such dark moments in life that he could not do anything other than cry and pray to God (Psalm 23). This mode of life could be one time or several times in a life, depending on personal situations. Natural or personal disasters could happen very few times in life if they happen at all. But other forms of life experiences can last for a long time or occur frequently, giving persistent pain and struggle. Some of the darkest moments of life are explainable by pointing out the source of evil. But other moments of life are hardly explainable because we do not know the cause of suffering. At other times, people face a time of darkness by their choice of wrongdoing. Still others, by their choice, willingly suffer for others.

---

1. See *Introduction* for the proposed concept of holistic transformation.

All of this painful experience has to do with the metaphor of *I am no-one* in the sense that I am broken: a broken spirit. This is a time when the sense of "who I am" is empty and does not make sense at all (like "nonrelationality" in Rosenzweig's term). This is also a time of enormous pain or erupting negative energy.[2] What is broken here is the sense of *I am some-one* and there is pain or yearning for the lost self. According to Freud, this broken spirit can be referred to as the "death-drive and life-drive" that creates a deep chasm in human psyche. According to Franz Rosenzweig, this *nothingness* or painful experience is related to the notion of "the meta-ethical self" that searches for meaning in the midst of impossibility.[3] This kind of metaethical self involves "a dense core of existential loneliness that in some sense is who we are."[4] This kind of self creates incessant birth of the self because of this deathlike experience. But this pain, the death-drive (Freud's term) or "death-driven singularity of the self" (Rosenzweig's term) is a moment of revelation in which the self is reawakened to the existence of others as others. When someone descends into a despairing experience (that is, *I am no-one* mode), he or she can feel the same agony of others. This aliveness to others, in Rosenzweig's view, makes one have a constant yearning for change and meaning of life in the midst of the unreasonable; and this is a moment when a divine revelation occurs to the self in the midst of *nothing* or chaos, because that could be the only moment of a revelation beyond current being so familiar with the present structure of power. It could be said that this is a moment when the self is ready for accepting a revelation.

This revelation moment arises with a dissolution of the superego, a giving up of pursuing a better self that follows norms or system of the current world. Because of a full dissolution in this attitude of *I am no-one*, a person is reborn with new eyes. This renewed understanding about self, neighbor, and God comes through moments of difficult life experience. In Rosenzweig's terms, this is a sparking moment of divine intervention of love, an ultimate source of energy that transforms "the world of social relations."[5] In a way, feeling shame or experiencing difficutlies creates a possibility of understanding a new world, precisely because of an isolation experience,

---

2. Sharon Welch similarly recognizes the power of rage or the role of human frailty in transformation. See Welch, *A Feminist Ethic of Risk*, 95–99, 178.

3. Santner, *On the Psychotheology of Everyday Life*, 77, 90–92.

4. Ibid., 72.

5. Ibid., 85.

A Transformative Reading of the Bible

which then gives critical, engaging space, not only with self but with neighbors and God. According to Santner, this strange experience of *I am no-one* is like being thrown out in an inhospitable, non-relational world, which calls for an answer, an urgent exit call from this chaos, and a mandate for a better understanding about self. This status of being thrown out creates yearning for solution in the midst of despair. The idea of *thrownness* in the world echoes the Heidegger's philosophy of *Dasein* ("being-in-the-world") with an emphasis on human finitude; yet, this thrownness should not be understood as an individualistic existence without engaging others.[6] This thrownness or strangeness in the midst of life is a moment of life when God is felt close.[7] It is also a moment of "my answerability to my neighbor-with-an-unconscious."[8] In the experience of "nothing" or *I am no-one*, the true face of "Other" emerges, even in a dim light.

From a political theological perspective, Santner suggests that we recognize "strangeness" in us and in others as well. This sharing of strangeness with others becomes a moral call to engage others, rather than a moment of making enemies or of removing strangeness. Furthermore, this strangeness is a moment of aliveness to God, and also to the very existence of who we are, which is perfected with the help of this alert strangeness. In talking about the importance of the presence of the Other in human transformation, Santner underscores the strangeness caused by neighbors or others (including God) because it becomes transformative energy:

> God is above all the name for the pressure to be alive to the world, to open to the too much of pressure generated in large measure by the uncanny presence of my neighbor. The peculiar paradox in all of this is that in our everyday life we are for the most part *not* open to this presence, to our being in the "midst of life." Everyday life includes possibilities of withdrawing from, defending against, its own aliveness of dying to the Other's presence. The energies that constitute our aliveness to the world are, in other words, subject to multiple modifications and transformations.[9]

Santner's claim is simple: Transformation takes place in the midst of ordinary, daily life. This is exactly what I argue, agreeing that human

---

6. Hans-Georg Gadamer critiques Heidegger's *dasein* when it fails to address the issue of others in the notion of *dasein*. See Gadamer, *A Century of Philosophy*, 22–23, 29.
7. Santner, *Psychotheology*, 9.
8. Ibid.
9. Ibid.

transformation is based on human experience (though I distinguish between three moments of life). When Santner puts Freud and Rosenzweig in conversation, Freud's death drive meets with Rosenzweig's metaethical self. Santner argues that miracles happen in the midst of life, not in glorious times as such, but in the most difficult times when we encounter "Other" or strangeness.[10] This moment of life can be understood as a moment of critical alert to oneself as well as to neighbor and God. In this mode of *I am no-one* the self is reborn in conversation with God and neighbors (enemies included). Of course this idea is not a traditional one, according to which "pain" (in the mode of *I am no-one*) or "too muchness" of life or "a surplus burden" of life should be *discharged*. This kind of psychotherapy based on cut-and-remove strategy comes from Freud according to whom this "too muchness" should be excised. While we have sympathy for Freud's concerns about this burden in his life context (where too much suffering or pain torments humans), we cannot think that this too muchness of life is simply avoidable or removable without appropriating it for transformation. Similarly, Levinas observes that too muchness of life characterized by shame can be a moment of transformation:

> The event of putting into question is the shame of the *I* for its naive spontaneity, for its sovereign coincidence with itself in the identification of the Same. This shame is a movement in a direction opposed to that of consciousness, which returns triumphantly to itself and rests upon itself. To feel shame is to expel oneself from this rest.[11]

This kind of transformation happens only when a person feels shame and turns it into a moment of engagement with self, neighbor, and God. Here begins a political theology that involves three subjects of transformation (self, neighbor, and God). The moment of *I am no-one* is needed in political theology because at that time human transformation occurs in relation to political life. The existence of pain or energy in this mode of "I am nothing" creates named or unnamed polarities (the strong boundary between friend and enemy), and also other polarities (the boundary between two modes of life—*I am no-one* and *I am some-one*), in the sense that the notion of *I am some-one* is broken. As two opposite polarities in electricity flow when connected, these polarities (strong boundaries between friend and enemy

---

10. Santner, "Miracles Happen," 76–133.
11. Levinas, *Basic Philosophical Writings*, 17.

and between these two modes of human life) may flow when connected with each other. This connection, metaphorically, means a difficult time of engagement with self, others (enemy), and God. There is a time of difficult relationship characterized by strange presence of others (what is hateful or shameful). What happens in this connection is a constant struggle with a dim hope of better understanding about self, neighbor, and God.

In this line of thought, the distance between "two modes of life" or between enemy and self is not great but is bridged in the mode of the self's engagement with others. Often the problem is that people do not recognize the enemy in themselves. The more serious problem is to remove the enemy and not to engage difficult neighbors and self (*I am no-one*). Unlike cancer cells, an enemy is not removed by force or operation because it permeates all our life in the world. It is impossible to separate personal pain from the world outside or from others. The only hope is to engage the enemy out there and inside of me. This mode of *I am no-one* also provides a moment of awakening to self, neighbor, and God in a new way. This mode of "nothingness" recalls the dust-made humanity in the creation story of Genesis 2. That is, while being thrown out to the world of tensions or meaninglessness, a person can awaken to the sense of "who I am" because of this "nothingness" experience—an attitude of humility. This sense of *I am some-one* is gained through the experience of *I am no-one*.

This kind of humbled, renewed person can identify his or her struggle or anguish with others. This then moves to the mode of *I am one-for-others*, not in the sense that I can help others because I have power or knowledge but in the sense that I can feel the same suffering of others. Through this nothing-like time, one realizes that he or she is dependent on God and on others—friend and enemy alike—for life. In that sense, dust-made humanity and difficult life experiences are not in vain and perhaps celebratory in nature because there is truth in living with the inability to transcend the ordinary life on earth. Put differently, this time of *I am no-one* helps one to understand that his or her life is not self-sufficient but interdependent not only with fellow human beings (including enemies) but with nature and God. An example of our thorough dependence on others or God is clear when we recognize that our life depends on farmers and God together. For instance, farmers work hard to grow rice for us; but we know that his or her work would be in vain without the help of nature. To our human life in general this truth might apply: our lives are dependent on others and God.

Theory of a Holistic Human Transformation

This dependence creates a humble spirit within us and a recognition that all members of the human community are to be cared for equally.

Transformation Cycle

In a transformation cycle having three modes of human life (*I am no-one, I am some-one,* and *I am one-for-others*), the moment of *I am no-one* is a central mode because this mode of life asks unresolved, perennial questions of why there is suffering in the world and why there are humans born with limits and vulnerability. Nobody can rightly explain the existence of evil or sin. What matters for us is how to respond to it. Our attitude about this "nothingness" is to accept what is weak or vulnerable in our human life. That is, through *nothing*, only through it, we know what life of *something* means, because the existence or interruption of nothing in our life, however painful it is, ultimately strengthens the sense of who I am. For example, when a person falls in the mode of *I am no-one*, his or her sense of autonomy or dignity is scattered and broken; but through this *nothing* mode (*I am no-one*), *something* (*I am some-one*) is reestablished in the way of placing hope in a broken world and is committed to living the life of *I am one-for-others*. Likewise, one can discern the meaning of true life in dust-made humanity through which the sense of self is renewed and reaffirmed. We are more than dust because we breathe (the breath of life); as a result, we become a living being (*nefesh*), which has both dust and the breath of life. This three-part human creation (dust, breath of life, and living being) reflects the three moments (modes) of human life (*I am no-one, I am some-one,* and *I am one-for-others*). Though the moment of *I am no-one* is decisive in feeding a transformation process, that moment alone does not make transformation possible. The three moments (modes) of life should continually take place in balance. Each moment or mode of human life has its own meaning and role, and each mode should not exist without other modes; it is a never-ending process. These three are placed in tension with each other and inform each other.

These three elements of human creation or three moments (modes) of life together reflect who we are (ontological-theological transformation), how we behave (psychotheological transformation), and what we should do (political-theological transformation). "Who we are" might be well explained and informed by the three modes of human existence (autonomy, heteronomy, and relationality); "how we behave" is well informed by the

A Transformative Reading of the Bible

three moments of life (*I am no-one, I am some-one, and I am one-for-others*) because these moments of life direct one's attitude toward oneself; "what we should do" is mainly informed by the three subjects of transformation (self, neighbor, and God). This kind of anthropological understanding of who we are, how we behave, and what we should do helps us to be aware of and be awakened to the existence of darkness, precious life in the midst of weakness, and interdependent networks of life in the world. It also helps us to engage our own *selves* in different moments of our life, difficult *neighbors*, and *God*.

In terms of a transformation cycle, we cannot presuppose that *I am some-one* is stable or stays forever as with the mode of autonomy presupposed in the Enlightenment tradition. Rather, it is given momentarily in response to *I am no-one* and *I am one-for-others*. It is vulnerable because of other two modes of life (*I am no-one, I am one-for-others*). As living being (*nefesh*), when we walk, we feel both dust-like life and smooth-breathing life. On the other hand, in this transformation cycle the mode of *I am one-for-others* is a mode of acting out or service to others; yet, this mode is not to be understood as that of "superman" who can do whatever he wishes; it should be informed by the other two modes of life. If anyone claims to be that kind of person without involving three moments of life, this moment of life (*I am one-for-others*) can be destructive to others because it does not engage others. Like Isaiah's answering call of "here I am, Lord, send me," it is not something that one can do because one is somebody but because one is called by God and accepts God's call to live the life of a living being (*nefesh*). Isaiah's call is one time but the renewal of his call occurs many times during his life. It is a never-ending process of human struggle and transformation.

However, this transformation does not happen to everybody automatically. Transformation can happen only when one goes through an extended process of engagement with "nothingness." Pain or suffering energy, created by a nothingness experience, is to be processed through an enduring prayer or reflection. As Edward Wimberly observes in pastoral counseling, the power of prayer works to delay some explosive emotions by helping the counselees to express what is necessary for their concerns.[12] As a result, the counselee begins to find healing, forgiveness, and reconciliation of the self, the world, and God. Otherwise, moments of life in such disasters could devastate anyone's life so easily and fast. The desire for speedy control of

---

12. Wimberly, *Prayer in Pastoral Counseling*, 99.

Theory of a Holistic Human Transformation

"nothingness" calls for a delaying process of in the mode of *I am no-one*. Here faith or prayer serves as delaying a sudden explosion of heat or energy due to *I am no-one*, and so it will prevent a premature closure of the process of transformation. Prayer means a process of communication with self, the world, and God through which experience of nothingness is controlled. Prayer, dance, psalms, or any other forms of faith activities might work in this place.

The analogy of nuclear fission will help us understand what it means to control the speed of the *I am no-one* experience in the process of transformation. Nuclear fission takes place when a nucleus is split *suddenly,* setting off a chain reaction. This break or fission can be said to be a kind of destructive energy. But when fission occurs slowly with speed control, it turns into useful energy (used in a nuclear power plant). A sudden breakup or explosion without speed control means, metaphorically, that one can be consumed by one's own hatred or pain from the mode of *I am no-one*. Similarly, this speed control is also important in political theology, as, for example, two polarities (friend and enemy) meet and explode without the process of engagement with speed control. Going through this gradual process of self-breaking in relation to the world and God, one can experience transformation of self. If the moment of nothingness is not controlled, as we can imagine in nuclear fission, the energy or heat caused by "nothingness" is destructive not only to self but also to neighbor. Metaphorically speaking, such a destruction may be comparable to the harm of radioactive material in the explosion of an atomic bomb.

This slow process of transformation through the mode of engagement entails anger, confusion, and frustration. But this is a time of divine revelation of a new love or new self that appears in the midst of a difficult time, even when the uncanny presence of others torments, or when *I am no-one* in the face of others and God. An example of this kind of transformation can be found in Hannah's story (1 Sam 1:1—2:11). Taking a long time of prayer without eating food or sleeping (going up to the temple at Shiloh year by year), Hannah goes through this kind of delayed process of transformation.

While the analogy of *nuclear fission* emphasizes the necessity of control in the midst of nothing-like experience, *nuclear fusion* underscores sacrifice of matter (the loss of matter), which explains the process of human transformation in a different way. In nuclear fusion, nuclei meet in high heat and pressure (this, metaphorically, refers to the mode of "nothingness"), and are fused with each other by losing some amount of mass, which releases some energy or heat. Loss of matter is sacrifice, and released energy is positive power to be used for others (like sunlight, which is a result of nuclear fusion). For example, Hannah goes through a difficult life (affected by high heat and pressure from within and outside of her). Under these difficult life conditions, what Hannah sacrifices seems to be her own (egoistic) self, which seeks her own son in the face of others (members of the community, and Penninah, her rival, second wife of her husband, Elkannah). Hannah probably thought her son would repay her troubled life and reward her in the future, even after Elkannah's death. Hannah prays that if God gives her a son, she will give him back to God. Loss of matter in nuclear fusion might be understood as her dedication of Samuel to God. The metaphor of nuclear fusion sheds new light on political theology in the way that nuclear fusion can be understood as a kind of "binding pain," which requires loss of something (loss of matter) under the condition of high heat and pressure. This loss of something means sacrifice of self in a certain way, taking the risk of being vulnerable to strangeness of others (including God) and merging with others. Theologically, this loss of mass also recalls the self-denial Jesus teaches in the Gospels. Jesus asks his disciples to bear their own cross to follow him. That cross is the life of voluntary sacrifice for others. "I tell you the truth, unless a grain of wheat falls to the ground and dies, it remains only a single seed. But if it dies, it produces many seeds" (John 12:24). The seed must fall and die; only then will there be many fruits. Paul also teaches that the problem of humanity in the context of self-centeredness and greediness is not to die. He asks us to die in order to live. In Romans 6:11, Paul declares, "So you also must consider yourselves dead to sin and alive to God in Christ." Similarly, Romans 6:3 says, "Do you not know that all of us who have been baptized into Christ Jesus were baptized into his death?" Paul's theology in the context of human self-centeredness and greediness is "die and live" not "die or live." Fallen leaves also teach a similar truth about self-denial or sacrifice. Leaves fall to fertilize roots of the tree. They are not a symbol of separation but a sign of new-life-in-death.

Therefore, what prevents genuine transformation is, in a sense, denial of sacrifice or denial of the difficult life, by generating fantasies against agitating fears or burdens. Fantasies are psychological apparatuses by which we keep forgetting the true nature of who we are in the midst of life. Fantasies create a separate world, always trying to escape the difficult world.

Utopia is created somewhere else than here.¹³ So deathlike life—voluntary or involuntary—should play a role in human transformation so that one can better understand who he/she is in relation to others and God. The cross is to be part of life: a) in terms of its message of comfort (solidarity) for those living the cross-like life "dying yet not destroyed" (2 Cor 4:7–11); b) in terms of its opportunity for personal transformative experience (like "death and life" together); and c) in terms of a political theological message of transformation through a harsh critique of the self and the world in the face of the self and the world not engaging the multiplicity of the cross.

Threefold Human Transformation

There are three aspects of human transformation: the psychotheological aspect with a focus on three moments (modes) of human life (*I am no-one, I am some-one, and I am one-for-others*); the ontological-theological aspect with a focus on three modes of human existence (heteronomy, autonomy, and relationality); and the political-theological aspect with a focus on three subjects of human transformation (God, self, neighbor).

The Psychotheological Transformation

The psychotheological aspect of human transformation has to do with one's internal change or renewal of mind and heart, when he or she goes through transformation with three moments of life balanced: 1) *I am no-one*; 2) *I am some-one*; 3) *I am one-for-others*. If one balances these three moments

---

13. For a long time in Christian history and discourse, there has been a tendency to deny difficult life experiences and so to try to overcome all sorts of dark periods of life, whether sickness or death. From Dante's *Divine Comedy* to modern-day televangelists' cheap teaching, there is a typical cultural syndrome of people imagining their life after death. They deny physical death to the degree that they produce the afterlife and view death as the enemy. In that view, death is viewed as unwanted and considered as a punishment of God because of Adam's sin. Let us ponder this. If Adam did not sin, would there be no physical deaths on earth? If that were the case, our planet would not have sustained so many lives up until now. It is impossible for humanity to live forever on earth. There is no clear textual clue that humans were created to live forever without physical death. In the creation story, the language of death can refer to a spiritual death in the sense that there will be no more communication and relationship between God and humanity because of Adam's sin. In the Torah physical death generally is not an enemy; it simply means cessation of life. At death people join their ancestors. There is no afterlife fantasy in the Torah.

of life, healthy transformation can occur. The point is that equilibrium occurs when all of these three moments or modes of human life meet and work together. See below figure 1 for the relations of three moments of life.

Figure 1: Three Moments of Human Life (Psychotheological)

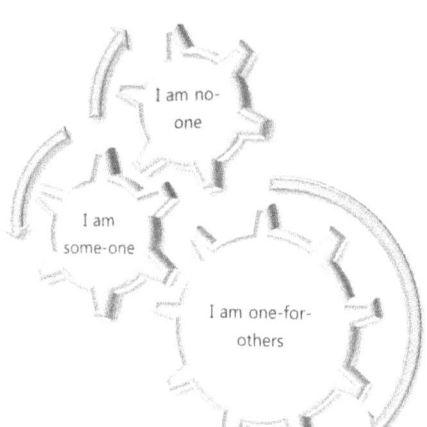

The Ontological-Theological Transformation

The ontological-theological aspect of transformation has to do with a person's ontological questions and ethics. For instance, the question is, who is "I" to the self, others, and to the community? Similar to the ontological-theological aspect is the political-theological aspect in that distinct political, theological questions are raised: for instance, what is the ideal relation between the self, the neighbor, and God? The ontological-theological transformation is understood as one's rendering of an ideal existence in the world, which has to do with balancing three modes of human existence (autonomy, heteronomy, and relationality). In a way, personal (autonomy) and public life (relationality) is balanced with each other in view of experience of others (heteronomy). So, with this kind of transformation, ontologically, one answers his or her call in the world, which is to live with three rules (rule by self, rule by community, and rule by others). This status of transformation does not require radical autonomy, heteronomy, or relationality at the expense of any of these. All these rules are equally important and negotiate with each other. So here transformation begins with the recognition that "I am I" (autonomy as singularity and sameness); yet "I am" is also incomplete without others (relationality) or the mysterious others (including the Other). On the other hand, this balanced life of three-rules-transformation leads to the ethical question of "how I should behave living with others in the world."[14] See figure 2 below for relationships between the three modes of heteronomy, autonomy, and relationality.

---

14. Moses's experience at the sight of burning bush (Exod 2:21—3:6) shows a good example of this ontological-theological transformation based on three modes of human existence. Moses (as kind of autnomous self) encounters the mysterious sight of a burning bush (heteronomy; the angel of the Lord appears), and turns aside to see why the bush is not burned up (a mode of engagement; relationality). Moses wonders why the bush is not burned up. The burning bush without being burned up seems to be a logical failure or beyond Moses's understanding of reality. This fact raises a serious question for Moses, who might associate this burning bush with the groaning and cry of the Israelites in slavery in Egypt, as the text implies (2:23–25). The point here is that Moses (the self or autonomy) does not jump into the burning bush (heteronomy) to see what is there but turns aside to see what is there (relationality). In this story we see three modes of human existence at work. He did not know what to do with this powerful, mysterious experience of the burning bush (heteronomy). Moses was unable to understand the meaning of the burning bush, which creates a mode of helplessness (*I am no-one*). Moses answers God: "here I am!" when God called him (Moses, Moses!). This is a mode of *I am some-one*. Through his critical observation and affirmation of God's call, Moses receives God's order by which he has to go to God's people to deliver them out of Egypt (*I am one-for-others*). God commands Moses: "Come no closer! Remove the sandals from your feet, for the place on which you are standing is holy ground" (3:5). "Come no closer!" suggests that there must be a fundamental distance between heteronomy (God) and autonomy (Moses). The earlier holy experience of seeing the burning bush is about the holy ground on which Moses should stand set apart to do God's work (to deliver his people). Heteronomy (the mysterious experience of God) faces a concrete reality, which is yet to be realized through Moses's work.

A Transformative Reading of the Bible

Figure 2: Three Modes of Human Existence (Ontological-Theological)

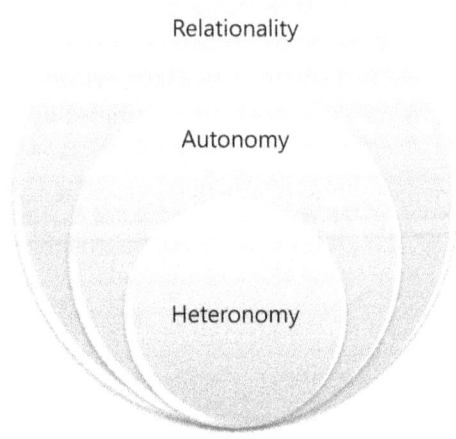

The Political-Theological Transformation

Likewise, the political-theological aspect of transformation takes a look at the three subjects of transformation (self, neighbor, and God) that involve the three moments (modes) of human life. For instance, the mode of *I am no-one* invokes a political response where "I am treated as no-one" by others or society. In such a moment, one asks: "Where is God? Why me (self)? Why are they prosperous (neighbor or enemy)?" These political, theological questions should be answered from the perspective of balance. That is, in political theology, these three subjects are to be involved with each other without bypass. For instance, the self's love of God can be dangerous to others if not filtered through the love of neighbor. In particular, the bypass of neighbor (or enemy) is a serious ethical, political problem, as the recent Korean movie *Secret Sunshine* shows. In it, a young mother struggles after her son is kidnapped and killed by a man in the neighborhood. Soon she becomes Christian through a local church's persistent evangelism that emphasizes "God loves you." Finally, she decides to forgive the murderer of her son and visits him in prison. While she is speaking to him, before yet offering forgiveness, he tells her, "I also believed in God, and God forgave me; so I am so peaceful now." This young lady is ever more confused and angry about such a God who forgives the murderer without her offer of

Theory of a Holistic Human Transformation

forgiveness to him. The movie raises the very question of love or forgiveness of God when there is no love or forgiveness involved between friend and enemy. In this movie the killer does not even ask for her forgiveness or show any regrets. The assumption is that God forgave him already; nothing else is needed. This is a difficulty with bypassing the love of neighbor or enemy. Likewise, in political-theological transformation, three subjects of transformation (self, neighbor, and God) should be involved with one another. This relationship can be seen below in figure 3.

Figure 3: Three Subjects in Political Theology

Now the most important thing is that transformation occurs simultaneously in many aspects as described above. The psychotheological, ontological-theological, and political-theological aspects of transformation are not separate or different but occur simultaneously even though the core of transformation begins with *I am no-one*, because this mode allows for one to see the truth outside of the self. The threefold transformation can be stated as follow:

A Transformative Reading of the Bible

The Threefold Transformation

Transformation	Self reborn with God	Awakening self	Relational self
Psychotheological	I am no-one	I am some-one	I am one-for-others
Ontological-theological	Heteronomy	Autonomy	Relationality
Political-theological	Self to God	Self to the self	Self to the neighbor

Horizontally, there are three aspects of transformation (the psychotheological, ontological-theological, and political-theological) in which three steps are involved. That is, the psychotheological aspect involves three moments of life: *I am no-one, I am some-one,* and *I am one-for-others.* These moments of life inform each other and are in tense balance. The ontological-theological aspect involves three modes of human existence: heteronomy, autonomy, and relationality. Likewise, these three modes inform each other and are in tense balance. The political-theological involves three subjects of political theology: God, self, and neighbor. Similarly, these three subjects inform each other and are in tense balance.

Vertically seen, we can name each column with a focus on transformative aspect of the self: self reborn with God, awakening self, and relational self. Self is reborn through "*I am no-one,* heteronomy, and God." Self is awakening through "*I am some-one,* autonomy, and new realization of true self." Self is radically relational to the degree that one can feel "*I am one-for-others,* relationality, and new realization of true neighbor." The foundational moment in human transformation is *I am no-one* through which the self is truly reborn with God and others. See below, figure 4, for the relations of this transformative self.

Figure 4: Transformation of the Self

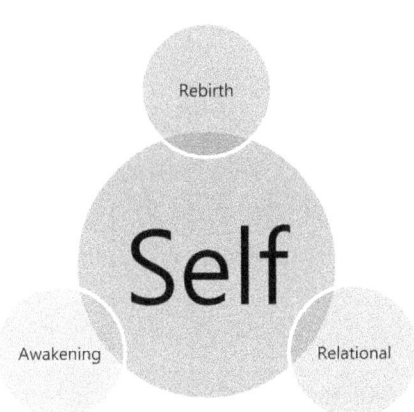

In sum, the holistic transformation requires us to change the view of transformation from static and linear to dynamic and circular, one that engages the self, the neighbor, and God. In the end, what I attempt to do in the following pages is to read select biblical stories transformatively in order to facilitate the reader's understanding of his/her own life in a similar manner. For example, Hannah's story can be read through the three moments of human life as she engages with herself, her neighbor, and her God. Here difficult neighbors, that is, her enemies, become a part of Hannah's transformation cycle as she experiences a change of attitude (*I am no-one, I am some-one, I am one-for-others*). In a similar way, readers may reflect on the parallels that exist between their own lives and Hannah's situation as she goes through her own time of transformation. In the next four chapters we will explore transformative readings of Hannah, Psalm 13, Mark, and Paul's letters.

CHAPTER 4

A Transformative Reading in Hannah's Story

THE STORY OF HANNAH in 1 Samuel 1:1—2:11 can be read in various ways: spiritual, theocentric, androcentric, or feminist.[1] Hannah can be read as a model of persistent prayer or piety (spiritual);[2] as a powerless person whom God empowers through grace (theocentric);[3] as a mother of the great leader Samuel (androcentric);[4] and as a woman whose hardships and shame are named and overcome, and whose active role of ritual offering is foregrounded (feminist).[5] Among these readings, feminist or emancipation hermeneutics exposes most concretely the ideologies of the privileged and advocates for the voices of the marginalized.[6] However, such a reading also has its limitations; the basic limitation is inherent in identity politics—"us" or "them" hermeneutics.[7] In reality, the world is much more complex—

---

1. Much of this chapter comes from Kim, "The Story of Hannah."

2. Augustine reads Hannah as a model of wholehearted prayer; Chrysostom links God's purpose for suffering to Hannah's spirituality. Chrysostom emphasizes the importance of prayer (piety): "You, then, woman, imitate her, and if you are childless, give evidence of this prayer, and appeal to the priest to join in making intercession for you; if you accept wholly his words in faith, the blessing of the fathers will result in lovely fruit in season" (quoted in Hill, "St John Chrysostom's Homilies on Hannah," 319–38).

3. Brueggemann, *First and Second Samuel*, 10-21; O'Day, "Singing Woman's Song," 203-10.

4. Evans, *The Message of Samuel*, 28-30.

5. Meyers, "The Hannah Narrative in Feminist Perspective," 117-26.

6. Tamez, *Bible of the Oppressed*, 53.

7. I use "identity politics" in the sense that scholars or practitioners advocate one identity against the other by making distinctions between oppressors and the oppressed, for example.

even among the oppressed exist oppressors.[8] Hermeneutically speaking, identity politics–driven hermeneutics has a relatively narrow conception of community but perhaps not as rigid a conception of community as other hermeneutical schools;[9] for example, the preferential option for the poor in liberation theology tends to exclude others who are not poor or marginalized in the community, just as oppressors exclude others on the basis of their social identity or privileges. However, through the lens of transformation, Hannah's story can be read very differently.[10] That is, Hannah's marginal experience can be understood as having transformative power.

Marginal, Transformative Identity

Marginal, transformative identity can be described as the self's dynamic, holistic process that involves transformations of self, community, and society.[11] According to the classical view, marginality or marginal identity is defined by a center and as such is viewed negatively;[12] a person of "in-between" culture (for example, between Korean and American) is seen as "a cultural schizophrenic"[13] or someone who has "a divided self."[14] In this view, the hope is to move from the older identity (or culture) to another newer, more secure identity. But this traditional definition of marginality is challenged by Jung Young Lee in his book *Marginality*.[15] He introduces

---

8. Debate over the issue of identity politics continues. Within feminism there is a wide spectrum of positions ranging from identity politics-driven feminism to postmodern Foucaudean feminism. In this chapter I am concerned with a specific branch of feminism that emphasizes identity politics. See McLaren, *Feminism, Foucault, and Embodied Subjectivity*, 1–17.

9. Conceptions of community affect our interpretations. In this chapter, I use a different conception of community that points to the vision of an egalitarian community for all, not characterized by identity politics.

10. By "anthropocentric" I mean to read the story of Hannah through her experience of *han* and marginality—not from a theocentric perspective.

11. Paul Ricoeur's *ipse* identity is characterized by selfhood that changes over time. This changing identity also has to do with narrative identity that involves the story of others. I expand the notion of "others" to self, community, and society. See Ricoeur, *Oneself as Another*, 21–31.

12. Lyman, *The Asian in North America*, 12. See also Stonequist, *The Marginal Man*, xvii.

13. Lee, *Marginality*, 46.

14. Stonequist, *The Marginal Man*, 217.

15. Lee, *Marginality*, 46–53.

A Transformative Reading of the Bible

three key concepts of marginal identity: "in-between," "in-both," and "in-beyond."[16] First, the experience of "in–between" (between two cultures, for example) is hard for the marginalized but it cannot determine "who I am." On the contrary, the experience of marginality can be affirmed as part of "who I am," and used as creative energy to contribute to a larger world. Second, "in-both" means that one can embrace both the old and the new place;[17] for example, one can become both Korean and American without negating either one. At this stage, the "in-both" of marginality can affirm "who I am" wherever I live,[18] not according to what others say I am. Third, "in-beyond" means that one can stay in both places and go beyond them. At this stage, one can identify with a greater community of all, beyond one's own cultural norms or comfort zone.[19] Seen this way, marginality can be redefined as having power to transform self, community, and society; it engages the world differently. This view of dynamic marginality can be applied to Hannah. She is indeed marginalized due to her infertility, but her experience of marginality, though difficult and/or negative, is not the last word for what she is about; she moves on, engaging her marginal identity and allowing for transformations to take place in the process of her struggle and suffering.

Furthermore, the marginal, transformative identity involves self-understanding of "who I am" in terms of life experience (or attitude) among which three moments of life or three modes of attitude stand out: *I am no-one, I am some-one,* and *I am one-for-others*.[20] The first person "I" implies that the self's view of life, or attitude, is important in transformations. The first moment of life is *I am no-one*, which refers to the lowest moment of life and the most humbling experience. *I am no-one* also can be understood

---

16. Ibid., 29–75.

17. The idea of marginality extends to a broader sense of marginal experiences, i.e., sociocultural life, religious life, and theological discourses. In that regard, "places" here can mean a variety of things: culture, identity, experience, thought, etc.

18. The primary identity of marginality is not determined by external elements such as race or culture. Here "in-both" means that the marginalized people should determine the identity of marginality.

19. Lee explores the meaning of marginality and its significance to Christian theology; he expands the theological insights of marginality to Jesus.

20. The idea of *I am no-one, I am some-one,* and *I am one-for-other* is based on my understanding of anthropology, which comes from my personal experience and a creation story in Genesis: that is, we are made of three parts, dust (*adamah*), spirit (*ruah*), and soul (*nefesh*); the first part informs the mode of *nothing (no-one)*, the second part, *something (some-one),* and the last part, *anything (one-for-others)*.

A Transformative Reading in Hannah's Story

through the experience of *han* (the Korean term), which is "the suppressed, amassed and condensed experience of oppression caused by mischief or misfortune so that it forms a kind of 'lump' in one's spirit."[21] This negative sense of *han* is a time of nothingness, and a time to search for meaning out of nothingness. The second moment of life, or attitude, is *I am some-one*; it is a time of awakening and self-affirmation from which one can declare: *I am no-one* is not "who I am." Similarly, a han-ridden person would not give in to the negative experience of *han* but would find a glimpse of hope.[22] The last moment of life, or attitude, is *I am one-for-others*, which is a time of commitment full of greater self-determinations. These three moments of life have roles to play in transformations of self, community, and society.

Hannah's Han

We need to grasp a deeper level of Hannah's *han* in multiple dimensions of her life—personal, communal, and sociopolitical. The first dimension has to do with her personal life, wherein her husband Elkanah cannot resolve her *han*. Elkanah is apparently a naively good husband.[23] He tries to comfort her: "Am I not more than ten sons?" But his comfort, in fact, aggravates her *han* because he does not understand the deeper side of Hannah's personal pain and struggle caused by Peninnah, Eli, and himself.[24] Elkanah as a male patriarch has what he wants—sons born by Peninnah, his second wife.[25] Hannah is the one who has to deal with a very personal dimension of *han*—anger, frustration, powerlessness, helplessness, and hopelessness. According to Amit, Elkanah shows indifference to Hannah's pain by neglecting her wish to become a mother, and is "guilty not only

---

21. Suh, "Towards a Theology of Han," 65. See also Ahn, *God in our Midst*, 42. Ahn puts it similarly: "*han* has unresolved deep feelings of anger, frustration and resentment of people who have become the objects of injustices upon injustices." Especially, Korean women's *han* is aggravated by patriarchy coupled with Confucianism's rigid social system as seen in the three principles and five virtues of Confucianism.

22. Chung, "'Han-pu-ri,'" 52–62. Like most *minjung* theologians, a Korean American feminist, Chung Hyun Kyung, for example, sees *han* primarily as negative—something to be overcome. But I consider *han* as having positive energy within it. Lee's "in-both" thinking alludes to this aspect of *han*.

23. Alter, *The Art of Biblical Narrative*, 82–83.

24. Amit, "Am I Not?" 73–76.

25. The text itself does not say that Peninnah is the second wife; Peninnah is believed to be Elkanah's second wife, based on the order of names: Hannah and Peninnah.

of insensitivity to his wife's feelings but also of disregard for her future" because "if the husband dies and the woman is left with no children" she has no man to support her.[26]

The second dimension of Hannah's *han*, which overlaps the first dimension, concerns her immediate communities, including her family. Hannah's *han* increases in the context of a double marginalization: the burden of bearing a male child for Elkanah and bearing public stigma in society. Hannah lives with the shame or stigma leveled against her because of a cultural frame that holds her responsible for the couple's inability to bear a child.[27]

The third dimension of Hannah's *han* has to do with the larger society and involves politics and religion. It is implied that the priest, Eli, is not doing his job well, to the extent that he cannot distinguish between praying and being drunk (1 Sam 1:12–14). When Hannah prays silently with her lips moving, Eli thinks Hannah is drunk. Eli, the most important religious leader in his time, does not know what is going on with her. It is an irony that Eli, who would have had a lot of experience with drunkards, does not distinguish between praying and being drunk. Maybe there was something unusual about the way Hannah prayed. Perhaps the crucial question is: if he thought she was drunk why he did not ask her the reason for getting drunk. Was she drinking her sorrows away? The implication is the same in either case: Eli's dull sense in reading Hannah's situation at the temple. Therefore, it is implied that there is a total crisis of leadership; a new, transformed leadership is needed, as implied in the Lord's judgment on the house of Eli where Samuel will replace Eli (1 Sam 2:34; 3:12–14).[28] Against this backdrop of a declining leadership—religious and political—it is not surprising that 1 Samuel begins with the birth story of Samuel. But the story of politics begins with Hannah, not with Samuel. There is no evidence that Hannah is less concerned about politics or religious matters simply because she is a woman desiring a child in the context of honor and shame or of the rivalry between herself and Penninah.

---

26. Amit, "Am I Not?" 75.

27. The text does not suggest that God is judgmental of Hannah's barrenness but in ancient culture a woman's infertility would amount to public shame and disgrace.

28. Actually, Eli's two sons, Hophni and Phinehas were "scoundrels" and "had no regard for the Lord" (1 Sam 2:12–17), which aggravates a declining leadership.

A Transformative Reading in Hannah's Story

The Three-Phase Transformative Process

The story of Hannah involves three moments of life experience as she undergoes the process of transformation: *I am no-one, I am some-one,* and *I am one-for-others*. Though the text does not say how long Hannah prayed when her family went to the temple at Shiloh, it seems clear that she prayed for a long time—for many years (they went "year by year" 1 Sam 1:3); Hannah does not pray only overnight or for just a few times. If we suppose that she has prayed through pain and struggling discernment, there must have been ample moments of life over a long period of time, including everyday life at home, in a community, and society. In other words, there is a long process of *han*-ridden life. Thus, we can safely divide Hannah's life experience or moments in her life into the three phases of transformation to which I now move.

The First Phase: I am no-one

I am no-one is a moment of life when her soul is severely damaged or ruined by oppressors or self-inflictions. She feels nothing. Peninnah provokes her: "you are nothing because you do not have a son, and God has closed your womb." In Hannah's time, if someone does not bear a child, it is a sign of misfortune; moreover, Hannah is responsible.[29] Thus, it is not difficult to imagine her agony and pain—her *han* deeply rooted in her own soul. It is a moment of life in which she gets stuck between herself and social expectations; society views her as worthless or nothing for her inability to bear a child. In a patriarchal society, no male means less participation in society; moreover, Hannah will be left alone without protection if Elkanah dies without children born by her. She also has to struggle with the issue of theodicy: "Why did God close her womb?" So Hannah weeps enough, struggles enough, and prays long nights and days, year by year (1 Sam 1:6–7). Every time Hannah goes to the temple of the Lord at Shiloh, Peninnah troubles her about her infertility. Furthermore, Hannah receives only one portion from Elkanah because she does not have a child. These facts cause

---

29. The story of Hannah resembles Job's story. Job claims he does not deserve such huge calamity and suffering. However, Job's friends keep coming, and insist that Job sinned and that God is right. His friends seem to say: "you do not know what you did wrong. God is not wrong. Repent. If you didn't do something wrong, your sons and daughters might have done wrong" (Meyers, *The Hannah Narrative*, 17–126).

her to lose her appetite; she does not eat or drink. That is why she seems to pray, according to Eli, with no voice—because she is enervated from the experience of nothingness.

It is also a time when Hannah has difficulty understanding the priest Eli. Why could a leader in the house of the Lord not appreciate what was going on with her? The text hints that the one who is blind or drunk is not Hannah but Eli; he is blind in a sense, not seeing what is happening in the temple. It is also implied that Eli has a dull sense of reading people and the community. Hannah's soul could be further saddened or broken due to the priest's insensitivity.

In this long period of struggle and brokenness, it should be noted that the text does not mention Hannah's resistance to Peninnah. There is no rivalry motif in the story of Hannah. Rather, she sets aside a special time for God, taking her *han* to God. In this time of nothingness, she expresses her *han*: "No, my lord, I am a woman deeply troubled; I have drunk neither wine nor strong drink, but I have been pouring out my soul before the Lord" (1 Sam 1:15, NRSV). The Hebrew phrase for "deeply troubled" is *qeshat ruah*. These two words mean, respectively, "severe, hard, harsh" and "breath, wind, spirit." Put together, the phrase can be translated "I am a woman whose spirit is hard" or "I am a woman who has had a hard time to breathe." In verse 10, Hannah expresses her situation as *marat nefesh* ("embittered soul"). She breathes with difficulty or a harsh spirit, meaning a lack of living being (*nefesh*). In a situation of *qeshat ruah* and *marat nefesh*, Hannah pours out her soul before the Lord. This pouring out of her soul reflects the experience of *han*.

Hannah's engagement with God continues: "Do not regard your servant as a worthless woman, for I have been speaking out of my great anxiety and vexation all this time" (1 Sam 1:16). It is important to understand her "anxiety and vexation all this time," which goes deeper than a mere personal level and should include the social and political dimension of her time, characterized by a lack of leadership. We cannot consider that Hannah would be unaware of this kind of malfunction of the temple and society; in other words, her great anxiety and vexation should point to the societal elements of her wish, which is to dedicate her son to the service of God for the community. In summary, her time of "nothingness" is certainly a time of soul searching, like being in *Sheol* (1 Sam 2:6), a time of questioning about God, and a time of understanding the community and society.

A Transformative Reading in Hannah's Story

The Second Phase: I am some-one

While seeking meaning in the midst of nothingness, Hannah asks of the Lord, and God hears her *han*;[30] it is a moment of something when she recovers the sense of who she is. Namely, she moves from laments of nothingness to the realization that "I am really no-one" before God (heteronomy); it is like facing the sun in daylight, which no one can do directly. Then, Hannah recovers a sense of self (*I am some-one*), and opens her eyes to God and sees a greater community of all.

This moment of "some-one" does not happen overnight but through a long time of prayer and struggle, as she undergoes a long process of gradual understanding about herself in relation to God and others. Hannah seems to realize a new time, a new space, and a new understanding about her, how she lives, how she sees the community and society from a different perspective. Hannah's sense of "some-one" comes only with a deep realization that *I am no-one* before God—an experience of lowly moments of life. Then, Hannah is reconnected to the spirit, the breath of God. Hannah's song in 1 Sam 2:1 shows a joy for life that shines brighter through the experience of *han*: "My heart exults in the Lord; my strength is exalted in my God. My mouth derides my enemies, because I rejoice in my victory." Hannah breathes smoothly again, despite her nothinglike *han*. Because of this "nothingness" experience, a moment of humbling and awakening, she recovers her self (autonomy), and continues to hold onto the rule of God (heteronomy)—the mode of heteronomous autonomy.[31]

The Third Phase: I am one-for-others

As a result of a long process of prayerful discernment, Hannah enters the mode of *I am one-for-others*—a moment of deep commitment and action; this mode is found in her prayer and offering at the temple when she takes the young Samuel to the Lord. She prays and vows: "If you give me a male child, I will give him back to you. I will set him before you as a Nazirite." Hannah dedicates Samuel back to the community and society from which she receives all kinds of anxieties and vexation, and which in return has

---

30. The name of Samuel could be a derivative of the verb *shama* ("to hear") and the divine appellative. Other possibilities include "he-who-is-from-God" (*shemeel*) and "asked of God" (*shaul meel*) (Cartledge, "Hannah Asked, and God Heard," 143–44). See also McCarter, *1 Samuel*, 62–65.

31. Levinas, "Dialogue on Thinking-of-the-Other," 204–5.

caused her *han*. Hannah's dedication of a child is more than a religious function in which Samuel is expected to perform religious duties in the temple. It is a religious and political action by which Samuel is expected to reform or lead society. Actually, the idea of Hannah's political action can be better understood against the backdrop of the political, religious dysfunction in the Israelite story. If Hannah is aware of religious, political evil done in the temple (the text suggests that Eli and his two sons are ill-performing) and society, what else could she give other than her son in that religious and political context? In addition, in a patriarchal society, where women's roles are so limited, Hannah's only viable option for renewal of society (or community) is her son Samuel who becomes an active leader for the following generations. In this way, Hannah is transformed, seeing beyond herself to a future leader who will fulfill her dream—a transformed community and society. Though she begins with "nothingness"—a bitterly broken heart of *han*—she does not give in to "nothingness." Instead, beyond (and through) her *han*, she dreams of a better society for all, which can be accomplished through her son.[32]

Notably, Hannah does not seek revenge nor to repay what she receives from her adversaries and society.[33] Instead, after a long time of prayerful discernment, she seems to know why she prays and what she seeks; it is a moment of immanence and transcendence; it is a new realization of "in-beyond" identity that conceives of the whole community. Indeed, Hannah's story becomes a model of personal and public transformation that goes beyond a personal level. This is a true model of public service that involves a holistic perspective—a viewpoint where love of self, love of neighbors, and love of God converge. The reason for and the purpose of her prayer is ultimately to give back what she receives; otherwise, meaning or transformation of self, community, and society would be incomplete.

Conclusion

In Hannah's life there are three things in balance: *I am no-one, I am someone,* and *I am one-for-others.* When "nothingness" comes, it is a time that

---

32. Meyers, *The Hannah Narrative*, 117–126. Hannah's expectation of her son's leadership does not imply that she is passive. On the contrary, she shows a strong public act when she brings Samuel to the house of the Lord "along with a three-year-old bull, an ephah of flour, and a skin of wine" (1 Sam 1:24).

33. Klein, *1 Samuel*, 83.

she is "hard of spirit." It is also a time of searching for meaning in self, community, and society. It is also a time of humility when she stands before God. Then, there comes a time of smooth breathing; it is a time of celebration of life when God hears her *han*. Finally, there comes a time of service to self, community, and society. These three things are not a one-time event or moment but recurring moments that involve transformations of self, community, and society. Likewise, the story of Hannah can illuminate our life stories in the way that we should live with these three states in balance. Through these three states of transformation (in Hannah's story), we recognize a broader conception of community that involves transformations of self, community, and society as a whole. As there is no separation between the three moments of life, so is there no separation between self, neighbor, and God.

CHAPTER 5

A Transformative Reading in Psalm 13

LAMENT PSALMS ARE BROKEN into two categories: personal lament psalms and community lament psalms. Usually, the latter have strong enemy-defeating verses (Psalm 3, 7, 12, 35, 58, 60), but the former do not. Likewise, the latter include a "punishment" statement within a petition, often in the form of "hear, save, and punish," but the former do not.[1] The communal lament psalms can be best understood through a political lens in the way that communal collective identity is more important than personal life experience or personal transformation. As sociological approaches suggest, crisis creates a need for a strong-bonded unity and requires a strong bitter enemy-defeating language. These communal lament psalms have their setting in national political crises so there is a strong enemy-defeating tone.[2] However, the personal lament psalms are different, with more focus on personal character or experience. This is because psalmists go through difficult lives, caused by various forms of lament (illness, abuse, death, oppression, etc), which may not require the same language of defeat or punishment found in the communal lament psalms. This, of course, does not mean that the personal lament psalms do not have feelings of animosity about potential enemies, persons, or other causes of lament. But the point is that they are part of the personal transformation process.

The personal lament psalms are more pertinent to the purpose of personal transformation because they contain personal life struggles, which can be identified with the three moments of life experience and three subjects of transformation (self, neighbor, and God). The personal lament psalms reveal three parties: "God, the one who laments, and the enemy."[3]

---

1. Westermann, *Praise and Lament in the Psalms*, 52–54, 74, 79–80.
2. Hopkins, *Journey through the Psalms*, 60, 74, 79, 83, 94, 129.
3. Westermann, *Praise and Lament*, 268.

A Transformative Reading in Psalm 13

These three parties are related to the three subjects of transformation: self, neighbor, and God. The character of lament Psalms "reveals an understanding of [persons] in which the existence of an individual without participation in a community (a social dimension) and without a relationship with God (a theological dimension) is inconceivable."[4] J. Clinton McCann also similarly notes: "the laments also teach us about identity—about ourselves, the world, and God. Psalm 13 holds together these three realms of experience that we are inclined to separate—the psychological (the 'I'), the sociological (the other/the enemy/the world), the theological (God)."[5]

Overview of Lament Psalms

The title "lament psalms" does not convey the character of these psalms in their entirety; in fact, they show a full range of emotions from lament to thanks to praise. Not fully understanding varieties of emotion in these lament psalms, we could too easily read these lament psalms with a *theocentric-individual* focus and not engage them with personal, political, and theological transformation in view. The typical reading goes like this: "in the midst of lament, seek God's help without stopping and trust in God, who will deliver you from all dangers or evil." As seen here, the problem is the absence of God; the solution is to get God's presence back on track; the method is to go through an earnest search for God. God cares for the elect and such a God is "my God." Otherwise, there is no dynamic role of self, which engages neighbor (or enemy) and God. For example, this kind of reading is well observed in James Mays's interpretation: "God's absence is the source of his anxious wondering in the face of the enemy's threat. The reality of God is such a crucial environment of his life that the psalmist cannot think or feel without thinking and feeling in terms of God's relation to him."[6] It is God who "hears and accepts complaints against him for lack of attention to suffering."[7] Otherwise, Mays does not consider reading the role of self, enemy, and God in view of transformation, especially on the lament's own transformational energy.

Walter Brueggemann recognizes some aspects of personal transformation that involve dark experiences both as part of the faith journey and

4. Ibid.
5. McCann, *A Theological Introduction to the Book of Psalms*, 93.
6. Mays, "Psalm 13," 279.
7. Ibid., 281.

part of human life.[8] For him, transformation refers to the life of seasons ("orientation, disorientation, and new orientation").[9] The weakness of his interpretation is that his view of transformation is linear, and he divides the entire Psalms into three moves: orientation, disorientation, and new orientation (or from trouble to search to solution).[10] But in my view, even the lament psalms, including Psalm 13 (a disorientation psalm according to Brueggemann), involve all three moves of orientation, disorientation, and new orientation. Furthermore, these lament psalms contain the full power of transformation because they involve all three moments of human life (*I am no-one*, *I am some-one*, and *I am one-for-others*). Transformation begins with a negative experience, as the lament psalms begin with lament. According to Brueggemann, negative experience (darkness) is to be discharged (likely in Freud's theory of talk-therapy) even though it helps one's faith.[11] But the energy of darkness is not merely something to be discharged; it is transformative.

Lament Psalm 13

1 How long, O Lord? Will you forget me forever?
How long will you hide your face from me?
2 How long must I bear pain in my soul,
and have sorrow in my heart all day long?
How long shall my enemy be exalted over me?

3 Consider and answer me, O Lord my God!
Give light to my eyes, or I will sleep the sleep of death,
4 and my enemy will say, "I have prevailed";
my foes will rejoice because I am shaken.

---

8. Brueggemann, *Message of the Psalms*, 52.
9. Ibid., 19.
10. For instance, James Mays put Psalm 13:1–2 in the category of trouble, vv. 3–4 of petition, and vv. 5–6 of thanks and praise.
11. Brueggemann, *Message of the Psalms*, 58.

5 But I trusted in your steadfast love;
   my heart shall rejoice in your salvation.
6 I will sing to the Lord,
   because he has dealt bountifully with me.

Psalm 13 is one of the shortest lament psalms; it has only six verses but contains all elements of lament psalms: description of suffering or lament, request, and praise. Generally, three moves are recognized: lament (vv. 1–2), petition (vv. 3–4), and trust (vv. 5–6); see the outlines below. The question is: how can we explain a move from lament to petition to trust? It is strange to see a radical shift of mood to trust in the form of past action ("But I trusted in your steadfast love"—v. 6). Is this because the psalmist remembered God's mercy in the past? ("God has dealt bountifully with me"—v. 6). Notice also that "my enemy" in v. 4 does not appear again in vv. 5–6. Why?

Formal Outline of Psalm 13

Lament (vv. 1–2)
"How long, O Lord? Will you forget me forever?" (v. 1a)
  a) How long will *you* hide your face from me? (v. 1b)
  b) How long must *I* bear pain in my soul, and have sorrow in my heart all day long? (v. 2a)
  c) How long shall *my enemy* be exalted over me? (v. 2b)

Petition (vv. 3–4)
  a) Consider and answer me, O Lord my God! (v. 3a)
  b) Give light to my eyes, or I will sleep the sleep of death (v. 3b)
  c) My enemy will say, "I have prevailed"; my foes will rejoice because I am shaken (v. 4)

Trust (vv. 5–6)
  a) But I trusted in your steadfast love (v. 5a)
  b) My heart shall rejoice in your salvation (v. 5b)
  c) I will sing to the Lord (v. 6a)
  d) Because he has dealt bountifully with me (v. 6b)

A Transformative Reading of the Bible

The above formal outline is helpful in understanding the moves from lament to petition to trust as experienced in personal prayer or worship. But the outline does not show transformation or how a person goes through various modes of life. Below is an outline of Psalm 13 attempting to demonstrate the movement of transformation.

Transformation Outline of Psalm 13

I am no-one—*a mode of heteronomy and a deep search of self* (vv. 1–2)
  Relation-less-ness and abandonment (v. 1)
    A remote God who does not answer (v. 1a)
    God's face hidden (v. 1b)
  Powerlessness (v. 2)
    Pain and sorrow deep in soul and heart (v. 2a–b)
    Enemy exalted over me (v.)

I am some-one—*a beginning of autonomy and engagement* (vv. 3–4)
  Sense of relation (v. 3)
    Hope of relation: addressing "my God" (v. 3a)
    Search of light (to my eyes) and life, not death (v. 3b)
  Engagement (v. 4): reason for engagement—because of injustice in the world

I am one-for-others—*awakening of relationality* (vv. 5–6)
  Awakening of relationality (v. 5)
    Because of *God's steadfast love* (v. 5a)
    Because of *God's salvation* (v. 5b)
  Sense of commitment to *the Lord* (v. 6a)
    Because of *God's mercy* in the past (v. 6b)

When we read this lament psalm from the perspective of personal transformation, we attend to the power of emotion, and envision the soul-touching experience in our life, both personal and public. This sudden storm-wrenching expression of lament has full life-transforming effects on a psalmist (or readers) because it engages at a time of a most difficult life experience, be it personal tragedy or any form of disaster or suffering. This transformative power of lament comes into effect when persons engage the process of transformation based on three moments (or modes) of life: *I am*

A Transformative Reading in Psalm 13

no-one (vv. 1–2), *I am some-one* (vv. 3–4), and *I am one-for-others* (vv. 5–6). In each of moment, God has a role to play. God, in the first moment of human life (vv. 1–2), receives complaints or laments and is accused of not caring about immediate needs. In the second moment of human life (vv. 3–4), God is addressed positively yet remains silent. In the third moment of human life (vv. 5–6), God is trusted yet again does not speak. The psalmist alone speaks and goes through his/her own transformation. Paradoxically, this seemingly absent voice of God propels the psalmist's cruel process of transformation.

Three Moments (Modes) of Human Life

I am no-one

As seen above, the psalmist begins with the mode of *I am no-one*, lamenting and feeling relationless or powerless because there is no answer from God. The suffering or pain caused by the enemy is severe and hard, especially when it lasts for a long time. So the psalmist cries, "How long, O Lord? Will you forget me forever? How long will you hide your face from me? How long must I bear pain in my soul, and have sorrow in my heart all day long? How long shall my enemy be exalted over me?" (vv. 1–2). In this moment of deep crisis, the psalmist is desperate for answers. The more urgent the answer, the deeper the pain goes. So "how long" seems to be forever, and yet God does not seem to hear the lament. There is no help but "my enemy" is exalted. This sense of *I am no-one* (relationlessness) contributes to the psalmist's anger, abandonment, powerlessness, and loneliness. As a result, the pain and sorrow accumulate and dormant energy rises. What option is there for a person going through this moment of life other than giving up hope?

Through the eyes of faith, this kind of despair can be a moment of engagement. So the question is realistic: What is God if he does not care? Does the psalmist have to trust in such a God? This moment of dilemma is crucial to a person's transformation process. Through meager faith in this time of total darkness, the psalmist begins to realize that this suffering is not the end of story but a moment when God is still present. In a way, suffering is another way of looking at the world and God beyond one's own calamities. Such a revelatory understanding may be possible because at this time of nothingness or powerlessness, one can realize one's own humanity as made of "dust" reflected in the creation story. It is an irony that this creatureliness has both a blessing and challenge. On the one hand, it is a blessing because when we are weak we can depend on God. On the other hand, we suffer! We are imperfect. Hopefully, in this mode of nothingness, one can see others facing the same dilemma of life.

Through the eyes of faith, enormous tensions and energy created by uncontrollable situations (something like Freudian *Neben*, or too muchness of our life) can lead to the power of transformation. As Rosenzweig suggests, this is a time of divine revelation—an awakening moment, not in the immediate sense of God's delivery from any suffering but in the sense of having a "faith-eye" that sees beyond the current harsh conditions of life. With Rosenzweig's insights, we can say that this time of "nothingness" provides an engaging moment with God in several ways: finding who God is, and who the self (the psalmist) is, and what the world is. This engaging moment is possible only because unwanted, devastating storms blew into the life of the psalmist. We can imagine the merciless storms hitting the Gulf of Mexico. Because of the storms the whole landscape of the Gulf of Mexico is being changed to facilitate a more abundant wildlife refuge. As we will see below in the next moment of life (*I am some-one*), the psalmist continues struggling because of this unpleasant challenge of storms, yet with a more positive sense of self. All in all, here in this moment of *I am no-one*, an easy solution is still far away; but the hope is yet to come because this is the moment of total dependence (heteronomy) that the psalmist cannot alter. The psalmist believes that God will not abandon him even in the midst of this devastation and powerlessness.

I am some-one

The mode of *I am some-one* means that the psalmist now searches for a positive solution because he sees a positive side of a relation with God and the world. So "my God" is a reclamation of a personal God. This is of the turning point for the psalmist who moves through darkness and sees a glimpse of hope that God is trustable, as in the past. No matter what happens in a person's life, it is not the end of the story. The psalmist seeks God's hand and protection. This is a moment of desparately seeking answers and protection: "Consider and answer me, O Lord my God! Give light to my eyes, or I will sleep the sleep of death, and my enemy will say, 'I have prevailed'; my foes will rejoice because I am shaken" (vv. 3–4). This is

A Transformative Reading in Psalm 13

a moment of engagement that asks for God's justice. The psalmist asks for "light to my eyes" because it is important to see the evil and suffering world in the exposing light of God. This light might refer to God's justice or love that shines on all people; God's light is impartial. Light to my eyes is the call of justice. The psalmist insists that if there is no justice, the enemy will say, "I have prevailed; my foes will rejoice because I am shaken" (vv. 3–4). The psalmist does not seek the defeat of an enemy but cries for God's justice and love. This mode of engagement is a reminder of how we are made of the breath of life (because life belongs to God and so it might symbolize godly communication). Because of this connection with God, the psalmist remains with God because he knows that there is hope—the hope that goes beyond current life conditions, something more than dust-made humanity.

Despite the search for an answer through positive engagement, the psalmist also continues to struggle with the nonsensical evil and inexplicable darkness caused by all manner of sources. The psalmist almost knows that there seems to be no outlet from this experience. Indeed, there is no way out without asking God to consider this situation. It is like praying: "Have mercy upon me and answer this difficult question: Why is the enemy prevailing?" This question will be answered when it comes to the discussion of the third moment of life, *I am one-for-others*.

I am one-for-others

The mode of *I am one-for-others* sounds promising to the psalmist. For the first time we hear the language of trust, thanksgiving, and determination. We cannot think of this positive language narrowly in the sense of "my victory" at the defeat of enemies (persons who cause suffering). Unlike the communal lament psalms, there are no punishment clauses or enemy-defeating words in this personal psalm. I argue that that is because the psalmist undergoes the process of transformation and realizes that the enemy is not to be defeated but to be included in the steadfast love of God. This reading is possible when the character of God, God's steadfast love, and salvation are understood rightly: Does *my God* hate or defeat my enemies? Does the psalmist trust in such a God? The psalmist's experience of *I am no-one* reconfigures his understanding of the world, God, and self in a way that a) the psalmist cannot help but call to God even though God does not seem to hear; b) the psalmist cannot avoid the existence of the enemy and the world he lives in; c) the psalmist learns how he is vulnerable or powerless in the world; d) the psalmist feels the double-edged sword of emotion: humility before God (because he can find in his own mind and heart the dark side of dust-made humanity), and frustration or anger because he cannot easily avoid or prevent the suffering or troubles.

In ways similar to electricity, the anger or remaining pain and suffering is transformed at this moment of *I am one-for-others*. Electricity flows from positive to negative. There are two polarities in connection. Similarly, our pain or anger creates two opposing polarities (me versus enemy). When these two opposites are connected like transformation power flows. How? This wire, metaphorically, can be understood as a time of engagement with self, the world (enemy included), and God. In this process of engagement, one can realize that the only way of hope is love and justice for all. If anyone still has an enemy, there is no peace. This universal love and hopefulness in the midst of hopelessness makes peace not only for the psalmist but for the whole world. If enemies are left behind or if anger is not dealt with properly, there is still separation, animosity, no peace, and no justice. This universal vision of a peaceful and just world is consistent with the image of God pictured in other psalms (God's righteousness).

The psalmist's renewed sense of identity that embraces the whole world leads to an expression of commitment and determination. The psalmist realizes that "I am more than *I am no-one* or *I am some-one*" because his life is meant to live for others too. Only then, he makes peace in the world. Until then, there should be some patience and lots of work. Three times an "I" comment indicates such a move: "But I trusted in your steadfast love" (v. 5a); "my heart shall rejoice in your salvation" (v. 5b); "I will sing to the Lord" (v. 6a). The psalmist now has a sense of a seamless view of time: past, present, and future. God is forever in the past, present, and future; so the psalmist trusted in such a God even now, and will do so by singing to the Lord.

The strong determination and commitment of the psalmist can be also understood in terms of his humanity as a "living being" (*nefesh*), who should live life in fullness. After the long prayer and search, the psalmist expresses positive statements of commitment to God's ongoing work: "I will sing to the Lord." This future thanksgiving and hope of God are consistent with the psalmist's faith: "but I trusted in your steadfast love" (v. 5a). The verb "trusted" is the present completed action, which means that the psalmist trusted in God even before anything happened, other than his internal change of mind and consequent renewal of hope. Enemies and the world are still there, tormenting the psalmist in one way or another, but the difference now is that the world and enemies are seen not as objects for removal because of pain, but rather, as subjects that need our understanding and engagement. The world and self are seen through the prism of God's steadfast love and justice. In this regard, the language of hope is more than a personal victory; rather, this hope yearns for permanent shalom and God's love and righteousness (*tsedaka*).

However, this yearning for or trusting in the steadfast love of God does not lead to naïve hope that all will be fine without engaging the difficult neighbors or enemies. The inclusion of enemies in the love of God does not mean that evil is allowed or that evil persons go unpunished. The point here is to emphasize an engagement from the perspective of holistic transformation. Until then, this psalm does not end. In this way, the psalm helps us to address difficult issues without losing faith in God, and to find a way out with assurance that God's love and justice anchoring our lives are bigger than ourselves.

CHAPTER 6

A Transformative Reading in the Gospel of Mark

CHURCH TRADITION IDENTIFIES THE author of Mark as John Mark, an interpreter of Peter and a mission companion with Paul (Acts 15:37–38). Yet, according to the Gospel itself, the author is anonymous. The author seems to be a Gentile Christian, living outside Palestine, based on the mistaken view of Jewish customs. The main audience seems to be a Greek-speaking Gentile audience who is not familiar with Jewish customs at all; there is the need to explain Aramaic words—for example, "Eloi, Eloi, lema sabachthani" (Mark 15:34). Some argue that the author might be a second-generation Jew, basically bilingual yet not fluent in both cultures (with less refined Greek and not a thoroughgoing knowledge about Jewish customs). Many scholars believe that the possible location of the gospel writing might be Rome. The date of writing of this gospel seems to fall between 65–70 CE when Nero's persecution took place and also when the First Jewish Revolt arose in Judea in 66–70 CE.

With this backdrop of the historical situation behind the gospel, we can say the audience of the gospel is mainly Gentile Christians who face strong opposition or threats from outside and inside of the community. The Roman Empire influences all areas of life with its propaganda of peace and security, and provides seeds of terror for Christians who believe in Jesus, not the emperor, is the Lord and the Son of God: "The beginning of the good news of Jesus, the Son of God" (Mark 1:1). Good news in Mark has to do with protecting and restoring the weak and the sick to their community. Jesus is the suffering Son of God who ushers in a new way of life. Therefore, in a hostile Roman environment, Christians have to choose between the way of Rome and the way of Christ Jesus. Furthermore, the Markan community asks: What is a desirable, meaningful life in this world when there is enormous suffering and injustices? What is a solution to human problems?

Overview of the Gospel

The Gospel of Mark begins with the good news of Jesus Christ, the Son of God and ends with the challenge of good news that requires difficult, costly witnessing. The Gospel can be outlined as follows.

Outlines Based on the "Good News" (*Euangelion*)

Beginning of the good news of Jesus Christ, the Son of God (1:1–15)
The power of the good news in Galilee and elsewhere (1:16—8:21)
Expansion of the good news and its challenge (8:22—10:52)
The price of the good news in Jerusalem (11:1—13:37)
The crisis of the good news (14:1—15:47)
The difficult news of resurrection and witnessing (16:1-8)

In the Gospel of Mark, Jesus Christ is mainly portrayed as the suffering Son of God who obeys the will of God even if it entails death, and proclaims the kingdom of God where all the vulnerable and social outcasts can be embraced. Jesus is declared as the Son of God at his baptism. After being tested by Satan, Jesus goes out to proclaim the radical kingdom of God and spread the good news of God to the people who need good news of liberation, healing, and peace (1:16—8:21).

As time goes by, this good news, though it is good and necessary for all, is rejected by some and creates tension and resistance from the religious leaders and upper class (8:22—10:52). Jesus knows about the cost of the good news and predicts three times that he must die. But his disciples never understand him; they are blind in a way (1:17; 2:14; 10:21). To signal the importance of true seeing, the section of 8:22—10:52 is framed by two healing stories of the blind men. In this section, Jesus emphasizes the cost of discipleship: "If any want to become my followers, let them deny themselves and take up their cross and follow me" (8:34).

Jesus' lonely journey continues even with opposition and misunderstanding. He cannot stop because the way of life is the way of the cross. Jesus confronts the authorities in Jerusalem (11:1—13:37). In Jerusalem

(14:1—15:47) Jesus, however, cannot save himself, and shouts for God's help and justice when he dies: "My God, my God, why have you forsaken me?" (15:34). He dies hopelessly. Good news seems to die too.

Then a young man appears in the tomb, bringing the good news of Jesus' resurrection. But women who visited the tomb are scared to tell anybody about the good news (16:1-8). Instead, they are stricken with fear and flee. Who can carry this good news to the people in need? The reality is this is difficult news to hear and bear because it entails cost. The story of Mark ends in this way.

Transformation in the Gospel of Mark

There are two kinds of transformation in the Gospel of Mark: Jesus' transformation in the narrative and the Markan community's transformation. The Gospel of Mark is read as Jesus' story. Thus it is possible to take a look at Jesus' own transformative experience. On the other hand, we also look at the transformative experience of the community behind this gospel.

Three Moments of Life in the Markan Jesus

Outlines of Three Moments in the Story of Jesus in the Gospel of Mark

***I am some-one* (1:1-13)**
  Prophetic confirmation (1:1-3)
  Jesus' baptism (1:4-11)
  Jesus' test in the wilderness (1:12-13)

***I am one-for-others* (1:14—13:37)**
  The Galilean ministry (1:14—7:23)
  The expanded ministry beyond Galilee (7:24—8:21)
  Jesus' journey to Jerusalem (8:22—10:52)
  Jesus confronts the authorities in Jerusalem (11:1—13:37)

***I am no-one* (14:1—16:8)**
  The Last Supper (14:1-31)
  The prayer on Gethsemane (14:32-41)
  Betrayal and death of Jesus (14:42—15:47)
  Resurrection and difficult news (16:1-8)

A Transformative Reading in the Gospel of Mark

As we see above, there are three moments or modes of life in the story of Jesus in the Gospel of Mark: *I am some-one, I am one-for-others*, and *I am no-one*. These three moments of life represent, respectively, a moment of blessed life with a strong sense of identity, a moment of committed life for others with strong will and action, and a moment of difficult life without hope. These moments of life are embedded with three modes of human attitude: confidence ("I can do it"), service ("I will live for others"), and humility ("Let your will be done"). If we focus on these moments of Jesus' life or modes of human attitude in the narrative, we may observe Jesus' transformative process or experience. Indeed, the Gospel of Mark emphasizes the humanity of the suffering Messiah, and therefore this gospel is pertinent to our study of transformation.

However, the flow of the three moments of life in the story of Jesus is different from that of Hannah. This difference has to do with genre. As the calling of prophets (such as Isaiah or Jeremiah) in the Old Testament begins with a moment of divine encounter, Jesus' story in the beginning of Mark begins with a divine call and confirmation at his baptism. Therefore, this kind of beginning is in the *I am some-one* mode. Hannah's story, however, begins with negative experience. The order of moments of life depends on the type of literature or on the purpose of storytelling. The climax of the story of Jesus in the Gospel of Mark is his suffering, which is the moment of *I am no-one*. In the following, we will explore the three moments in the story of Jesus.

I am some-one (1:1–13)

The Gospel of Mark begins with a bold claim about the good news (*euangelion*) of Jesus Christ. John the Baptist in the wilderness prepares for Jesus' coming in ministry with power. Jesus is the one who is promised by the prophet Isaiah. At his baptism, Jesus is announced the Son of God ("this is my beloved Son; I am well pleased with him") with a sign of the heavens *torn apart* and a symbol of a dove descending onto him. This is God's Son, a glorious title with attached privilege (*I am some-one*). This baptism can be a similar experience of prophetic calling of the Old Testament in the sense that God appears to confirm one's vocation. Jesus' vocation has to do with a voice from heaven: "You are my Son, the Beloved; with you I am well pleased" (1:11). In the Old Testament context, God's son is either the one who works for God (king, prophet) or the whole of Israel collectively as God's son (children). In this voice, Jesus is declared to do God's work as God's Son.[1] Jesus is singled out and he is *I am some-one* because of God's confirmation. In the Roman Empire, an emperor's enthronement displays various symbolic forms of divine confirmation and popular support. So Jesus as God's Son, not Caesar of the Empire, is a bold claim and comes with the sense of strong identity.

But signs of heaven torn apart and a dove descending on Jesus are significant in the narrative of the Markan Jesus. These signs are striking because we know that eventually at Jesus' death the temple curtain is torn apart. This curtain might represent the symbolic division or separation between those who have power and those who do not. The original idea of the temple curtain is to give loyalty to God only. But when this curtain serves the purposes of ethnocentrism or religious exclusivism, it is torn apart. Jesus' act of good news collapses such a boundary. As a result, a dove, a symbol of peace, descends on Jesus. Put differently, early on at Jesus' baptism, his future mission is implied here with two signs: boundary-breaking and peacemaking. It is also striking that Jesus, the Son of God, is led by the Spirit to the wilderness and tested by Satan. This test symbolizes his participation in God's liberation of his people in the story of Exodus.

I am one-for-others (1:14—13:37)

Right after Jesus' baptism and test in the wilderness, he begins his public ministry in Galilee and elsewhere. This is the time of *I am one-for-others*. The first phase covers his Galilean ministry of healing and teaching (1:16—7:23). Jesus teaches with power and authority, unlike those who teach by words only. Many people are surprised by his teaching, impressed by his power of healings of the sick and the downtrodden. Jesus, being confident of his call and ministry, continues to work for others. People gather around, in the desert and at the sea and press on to him to hear more about good news and to receive blessings (that is, real good news). At the sea of Tiberia he teaches even at the boat because of the crowd's pushing in on him. So far, so good; there is no opposition against Jesus. Miracles are performed to let people know about his identity, power, and compassion for other people. Jesus proves that he is the powerful Son of God. He feeds five thousand and four thousand in the desert only with a few loaves of bread and a few fish.

1. Dowd and Malbon, "The Significance of Jesus' Death in Mark," 271–97.

But truthfully, people who praise Jesus' powerful ministry here in Galilee and elsewhere never fully understand the price of the good news. Jesus' disciples do not understand either. Jesus knows about the price of this good news because he knows that some people (religious leaders and other political elites) do not like his message and deeds.

In the second phase of his ministry (7:24—8:21), Jesus expands to the area of Gentiles. *I am one-for-others* includes Gentiles. The Syro-Phoenician woman is included in the love of God. Initially, Jesus rejects the request of this woman, based on his identity and understanding of ministry to Israel only. But he is confronted and recognizes the necessity of this woman's request. His sense of *I am one-for-others* is certainly expanded.

While Jesus does great things in his public ministry, people hardly understand who he is other than a miracle-worker. Jesus decides to go up to Jerusalem, the center of religion and politics, to challenge religious leaders to follow God's way (8:10—10:52), whereas his disciples are preoccupied with greater seats they might get in the new kingdom of God. Finally, Jesus confronts the authorities in Jerusalem (11:1—13:37). This is a very dangerous time for Jesus. He could have stayed in Galilee, teaching with power, performing miracles. He could have been a hero of a local people. But his sense of call and his sense ministry refuses this boundary. Rather, his ministry is breaking boundaries or any religio-social conditions that prevent people from living just, peaceful lives.

I am no-one (14:1—16:8)

At chapter 14 the tone of the story turns dark; its pace is fast, leading to the death of Jesus. Jesus eats the last supper with his disciples. He knows he will not be eating or drinking again with his disciples. With a conflicted mind Jesus goes to the mountain Gethsemane to pray with his disciples (14:32–41). Jesus prays, "Abba, Father, if you can, remove this cup from me." This is a moment of intimacy and trembling. God is called "Abba," and Jesus might expect to receive something favorable or to hear good news. Instead he is shown the way of cross. In this moment of *I am no-one* Jesus cannot save himself from this way. I am suggesting this is not the only moment of *I am no-one* in the story of Jesus in the Gospel of Mark but it is the climax of these moments of *I am no-one*. Jesus, the Son of God, who was lauded by God at his baptism ("You are my Son") does not look like a beloved son any more because he cannot escape this dark moment by himself. Jesus' beloved Father does not answer him. He prays three times and comes back to his disciples only to find, to his disappointment, they all are asleep. God's Son Jesus is struggling and does not want to die for the world. Jesus seems to ask: "Why me? Remove this cup from me." After many moments of fear, Jesus gives in to God's will (*I am no-one*) and prays "your will be done."

Betrayal and interrogation follows him. Jesus dies on the cross and cries in desparation (14:42—15:47). His last cry on the cross is not only the cry of bitterness but the cry for the justice and love of God: "My God, my God, why have you forsaken me?" (Ps 22:1). This God is no more called Abba, but "my God," which is used in psalms when a psalmist cries for God's help and justice in the midst of injustice and chaos. Jesus' cry for help and justice is final realization that he cannot do anything; it is a moment of *I am no-one* (heteronomy) and asks for God's intervention. This is an irony and a shock for those who remember that Jesus is someone special, the powerful Son of God who performs miracles and healings. In Mark, Jesus' suffering is difficult to bear.[2] But Jesus goes through such an ordeal because of God's will. When he obeys God's will, God vindicates him. Jesus becomes a model of righteousness because of his faith in God.

Transformation in the Markan Community

As indicated earlier, the Markan community, probably living in Rome under Nero's rule, faces issues on multiple fronts, among which the gravest things are how to live in a hostile, persecuting environment where people are self-centered and sacrifice others for their own interests. During this time in Rome there were lots of multiethnic Christians, Jews and Gentiles, immigrants and locals. The Markan community is taught to serve the weak and the marginalized. Members are called by God and experience the mercy of God. This new kinship-based community of God gives them a sure identity in God through Jesus. It is a period of *I am some-one*. These young Christians are confirmed as God's people.

As newly adopted children of God, members of the Markan community are full of energy and confidence. This is a time of *I am one-for-others*.

---

2. This picture of Jesus' cross in the Gospel of Mark is very different from that of Luke's or John's. According to Luke, Jesus is adamant about his mission and realtively calm about suffering and crucifixion. There is no lament. Instead, he prays: "Father, forgive them . . . I commit my spirit to you." The Gospel of John portrays Jesus' death as a moment of glory, nothing lamentable but something joyful in a certain sense.

As Christian works and teachings spread, more people know about the Christian faith. Then, like Jesus, this community also faces severe challenges, as it expands ministry to other areas. As time goes by, this community faces severe persecution or internal conflicts or interreligious conflict between Jews and Gentiles. As with Peter's betrayal of Jesus in the story of Mark and the disciples' lack of understanding about Jesus, this community's understanding of Jesus has become dull. The sense of strong identity is shaky because of internal and external challenges to this young community. Just as local and Jerusalem leaders challenge Jesus, Mark's community is directly threatened by social-political powers in Rome.

And just as Jesus cannot do anything on the cross, this community feels nothingness, powerless, hopeless. Like Jesus' death on the cross, the community seems to tremble and shout for justice without seeing miracles in sight. It is a bitter cry of nothingness. Even God seems absent in this very moment when the community needs help. It is a moment of total despair for this community, as no miracles happen. Faith only seems to invite more evil and death. Jesus' disciples flee from the cross, many of Mark's community flee from imperial threats. People in the Gospel do not understand who Jesus is; likewise, no one in Mark's community truly understands Jesus anymore.

As we see here, the Markan community's life is reflected in this story of Jesus. As Jesus is powerless on the cross, so this community is powerless. As disciples hardly understand Jesus' mission or good news, this community is no exception. In the end, the readers hear the rhetorical question: Are you the women in the tomb fleeing out of fear? It is hoped that the hearers of this gospel undergo transformation as they respond to the narrative and see Jesus' own transformative process as he yields to God's will. Transformation means a change of view of self. With this renewed sense of who they are, how to live, and for whom, this community can continue to live according to the good news preached in the gospel. In fact, the Gospel of Mark emphasizes not believing in Jesus but believing in good news (1:15) or believing in God (11:22) who sent Jesus for the sake of his little children (the weak, poor, marginalized). So Jesus says: "Whoever welcomes one such child in my name welcomes me, whoever welcomes me welcomes not me but the one who sent me" (9:37). Extended kinship is a vision for this community: "Who is my mother and my brothers? Whoever does the will of God is my brother and sister and mother" (3:35).

A Transformative Reading of the Bible

The final challenge to the community is reflected in the story of the women fleeing the tomb. What if the members of the community were in the position of these women who heard and witnessed good news of the risen Lord and failed to tell this news to anyone? The last scene of the Gospel of Mark is open-ended. Mark's readers are invited to ask and answer the question What could they do? The Markan community can grow and continue its faith through the cyclic process of transformation: from *I am some-one* to *I am one-for-others* to *I am no-one*. But this is not a linear process; it is circular. Because of an *I am no-one* experience, now members of the community are reawakening to the grace of God and are empowered through the suffering Son of God who goes through the life of obedience to God's will. The moment of *I am no-one* also gives momentum to their identity as ones meant to serve others, as Jesus lived the life for others: "For the Son of Man came not to be served but to serve, and to give his life a ransom for many" (Mark 10:45).

CHAPTER 7

A Transformative Reading in Paul's Letters

LIKE IN THE CASE of the Gospel of Mark, we can think of at least two kinds of transformation in Paul's letters: Paul's own transformative experience and the believers' transformation. Paul's own transformation will be looked at through Galatians, 1–2 Corinthians, and Romans. Believers' transformation will be investigated through 1 Cor 4–11 and Rom 1–15 in particular.

Paul's Ministry in Context

In order to understand Paul's ministry, we will consider three things: Paul's view of time, Christ, and Judaism.[1] First, Paul believes that the new time has dawned through Christ Jesus and that this new time will be completed at the end "when he hands over the kingdom to God the Father, after he has destroyed every ruler and every authority and power" (1 Cor 15:24). This new time also should be understood in terms of quality of life in the present when Christian members find Christ in their lives: "There is no longer Jew or Greek, there is no longer slave or free, there is no longer male and female; for all of you are one in Christ Jesus" (Gal 3:28). If anybody belongs to Christ, he or she is "Abraham's offspring, heirs according to the promise" (Gal 3:29). In addition, this new time is set against the ideology of the Roman Empire that seeks not God's kingdom but its own glorious kingdom at the expense of the weak and the marginalized. This new time by Christ exposes all kinds of human arrogance, ideology, and all forms of unfaithfulness to God and to fellow human beings. In a nutshell, the goal of the new time is to bring God's righteousness in the world.[2] In the wider Roman and Jewish context of Paul's life and ministry, it is God's righteousness

1. Kim, *A Theological Introduction to Paul's Letters*, 15–22.
2. Ibid., 38–62.

A Transformative Reading of the Bible

that matters, not our own righteousness. God is the one who is righteous and promises Abraham and all his descendants that they will be blessed. In view of Paul's familiarity with the Jewish scripture and theology, "the righteousness of God" in Romans 1:17 or in 3:21–22 is understood as God's covenantal faithfulness to his promise.

Second, Paul changes his view of Judaism and extends the covenantal framework to include the Gentiles. Formerly, Paul thinks that the God of the Jews is for them only, but now he corrects that view, believing that the same God of the Jews is also the God of the Gentiles (Rom 3:29). Otherwise, Paul never left Judaism or misunderstood the law; rather, he says, "the law is holy" (Rom 7:12) or "the law is spiritual" (Rom 7:14). He asks: "Has God rejected his people? By no means!" (Rom 11:1).

Third, Paul changes from his former view of the messiah according to which Christ crucified cannot be the messiah at all. He now believes that Jesus Christ crucified is Israel's long-awaited messiah, although most of his fellow Jews do not accept such a messiah. Now the very Christ crucified is the messiah for him. He found that Christ Jesus as the messiah showed his faith in God to bring God's righteousness to the world by dying on a cross.[3] Paul finds that Christ fulfills the law (Rom 10:4) whose goal is to honor God and to bless humanity. Christ embodies this law of God (equivalent with God's righteousness). Otherwise, Christ does not repeal the law because it convicts people or it is impossible for people to earn righteousness. Rather, Paul emphasizes the law of faith (the law of God) against the law of sin by which people seek their own glory.

In Paul's mind, this kind of Christ crucified is everything. Paul's life is soaked with Christ experience, especially Christ's death and love, as he says in Gal 6:14–16: "May I never boast of anything except the cross of our Lord Jesus Christ, by which the world has been crucified to me, and I to the world. For neither circumcision nor uncircumcision is anything; but a new creation is everything!"

So Paul has a long journey of thorns and thistles on his way to the living Christ, as he says that "from now on, let no one make trouble for me; for I carry the marks of Jesus branded on my body" (Gal 6:16). In a way he summarizes his life and sense of who he is very well in 1 Corinthians 15:9–10: "For *I am the least of the apostles*, unfit to be called an apostle, because I persecuted the church of God. But *by the grace of God I am what I am*, and his grace toward me has not been in vain. On the contrary, I

---

3. Ibid., 63–82.

worked harder than any of them—though it was not I, but the grace that is with me. Whether then it was I or they, so we proclaim and so you have come to believe."

As we see here, his understanding of the three moments of life is well reflected. Philemon 3:7–9 also testifies about how he understands himself in view of his Christ experience: "Yet whatever gains I had, these I have come to regard as loss because of Christ. More than that, I regard everything as loss because of the surpassing value of knowing Christ Jesus my Lord. For his sake I have suffered the loss of all things (*I am no-one*), and I regard them as rubbish, in order that I may gain Christ and be found in him (*I am some-one*), not having a righteousness of my own that comes from the law, but one that comes through faith of Christ (*I am one-for-others*), the righteousness from God based on faith."

Paul's Transformative Experience (Gal, 1–2 Cor, Rom)

Paul's transformative life experience converges in his understanding of three moments of life as he states well in 1 Cor 15:9–10 and Phil 3:7–9. At the center of this kind of balanced understanding is his experience of Christ—his life and death. In every place he visits, the basic message is the same: it is Christ crucified (1 Cor 1:23; 2:2; Gal 6:14), which gives him transformative experience. So he asks others to join him. In fact, as for Paul, Christ is the one who goes through these three moments of life: *I am no-one* (in his suffering and death), *I am some-one* (as God's Son), and *I am one-for-others* (in his life and death living for others). "Christ became obedient to the point of death, even death on a cross" (Phil 2:8).

Christ's suffering and death serves as a central mirror or metaphor through which Paul sees himself, the world, and God.[4] The importance of this lens is well stated in Gal 6:14–15: "May I never boast of anything except the cross of our Lord Jesus Christ, by which the world has been crucified to me, and I to the world. For neither circumcision nor uncircumcision is anything; but a new creation is everything!" It is Paul's understanding that the world (as a collective term of all people and systems in society) as a living entity is crucified by the cross of Jesus Christ, so that the world of

---

4. This kind of understanding about Paul's theology is called "a threefold theology of Paul." See Kim, *A Theological Introduction to Paul's Letters*. Namely, Paul's theology is operative with the following three aspects: God's righteousness, Christ's faith, and the believer's participation in Christ. See also Kim, *Christ's Body in Corinth*.

injustice, unfaithfulness, and all forms of evil acts may no longer propogate other forms of crucifixion of innocent people. Yet another reason for the world's crucifixion is the world's voluntary sacrifice *for others*, as Christ's cross implies. This world (as cosmos) cannot be separated from everyone's existence. That is why Paul states this crucifixion of the world by the cross of Jesus is done "to me" (Paul). This "to me" is his living of Christ crucified, through which he sees self, the world, and God. That is, God loves the world (God's righteousness is revealed) and Christ showed his love until he died on a cross (Christ's faithfulness) for the world. Yet the world remains unchanged even though the new time has dawned now through Christ's faithfulness. This logic is certainly possible. As a Jewish thinker, Paul believes that God is the creator of good creation and God still cares about this world. In Romans, Paul clearly connects the groaning of the world because of sinful acts of humanity. The cosmos as a whole is the target of God's mission and Paul's concerns. There is no separation between the world and humanity or between the world and any other beings or nature. It is altogether God's good creation. In this regard the world's crucifixion makes sense. In the same vein, we can understand his statement of "his crucifixion *to the world*" in the sense that he is committed to serving the world through the lens of crucifixion. He is to live Christ crucified. So he goes through difficult times of suffering and persecution because of his commitment to the world. This commitment to the love of the world makes possible his life of crucifixion. He so lives with this statement: "I die everyday!" (1 Cor 15:31).

This reading lens of Paul has to do with the mode of *I am no-one* because of Christ's love and sacrifice. This *I am no-one* means two things for Paul. One is his life of sacrifice in the midst of injustices and persecutions. He is treated like nothing by the world. The other is his thorough sense of who he is before God and others. He says: "I am the least of these apostles . . ." Once he was impressed with the power of the gospel, he regarded all he knew as nothing. So this means, relatively speaking, nothing is comparable to the love of God or the love of Christ. His attitude toward God (it is only God's grace that allows who Paul is) and toward others, including the Jerusalem apostles, is humility. Once he thought he was "some-one," born with good lineage along with an honorable educational background, but now he truly feels this understanding is naïve because he did not appreciate the love of God for all people, and the universal implication of Christ's faithfulness for all people.

A Transformative Reading in Paul's Letters

In this "no-one" mode of life, like Christ, Paul confronts the suffering and evil in the world, and risks his life because of the love for the world, God, and Christ. Along the way, he undergoes perils, his own vulnerability or physical weakness, persecution, and even near-death moments because of the gospel of Christ. For Paul, all this nothingness experience (death or persecution) cannot be avoided but can be transformed into making God's love or God's righteousness revealed, as Christ reveals it.

Three Moments of Life in Paul's Transformation

Paul's three moments of life are stated here in 2 Cor 4:8–12:

> We are afflicted in every way, but not crushed; perplexed, but not driven to despair; persecuted, but not forsaken; struck down, but not destroyed; always carrying in the body the death of Jesus, so that the life of Jesus may also be made visible in our bodies. For while we live, we are always being given up to death for Jesus' sake, so that the life of Jesus may be made visible in our mortal flesh. So death is at work in us, but life in you.

The mode of *I am no-one* is seen in verses 8–9a; *I am some-one* is in 9b-10; and *I am one-for-others* is in 11–12. *I am some-one* because *I am no-one* ("carrying in the body the death of Jesus, so that the life of Jesus may also be made visible in our bodies"). At the same time, *I am one-for-others* because one lives to be "given up to death for Jesus' sake" (v. 11). As a result, "death is at work in us, but life in you" (v. 12). When we die, we live and you live. This teaching is very consistent with Rom 6:11 ("Dead to sin *and* alive to God in Christ Jesus").

Because of this experience of Christ, Paul urges and comforts the Philippians, for example: "Only, live your life in a manner worthy of *the gospel of Christ*, so that, whether I come and see you or am absent and hear about you, I will know that you are standing firm in one spirit, striving side by side with one mind for *the faith of the gospel*" (Phil 1:27). The gospel of Christ and the faith of the gospel are interchangeable, and their meaning can be best understood in the context of Christ's death and crucifixion. If this is so, Phil 1:29–30 makes good sense; Paul states that suffering for Christ is needed: "For he has graciously granted you the privilege not only of believing in Christ, *but of suffering for him as well*—since you are having the same struggle that you saw I had and now hear that I still have."

A Transformative Reading of the Bible

More specifically, Paul gives us his understanding about himself as he begins writing Romans. We see his sense of "I am some-one" in 1:1,—"Paul, a slave of Jesus Christ, called to be an apostle, set apart for the gospel of God." This call for the gospel of God is "the gospel concerning his Son" (1:3). The gospel of God can be understood as God's righteousness in Rom 3:21–26 where *dikaiosyne theou* (the righteousness of God) can be read as "God's own righteousness" (the subjective genitive). Then the gospel of Christ means the Son embodies this righteousness through his faithfulness (*pistis christou*), which leads to suffering and even death on a cross.

Paul's sense of *I am some-one* is not based on a Jerusalem connection or on patrons' support. Rather, it is based on his experience of God's love through Christ's faithfulness. This understanding of himself as someone special is never to be understood as separated from *I am no-one*. In addition, at the same time, this sense of *I am no-one* and *I am some-one* should lead to a cross-carrying life.

But if there is no balance between these three modes of life in Paul's churches, Paul advises his communities to stay in such a balance. Similarly, in such a situation, Paul's local congregations also seek Paul's council to deal with all kinds of disruptive, disembodying ideologies and practices in their communities. For example, if Christian Jews claim that Gentiles should be circumcised to become children of God (special status of *I am some-one*) without understanding the meaning of Christ's sacrifice or faith, according to Paul, circumcision or noncircumcision does not matter because what really matters is "the law of faith, not the law of works" (Rom 3:27) or "the law of God, not the law of sin" (Rom 7:25), through which God's righteousness is revealed (Rom 3:21–26). While Paul does not negate the place of Israel (Rom 9–11), what he says is that the mode of "I am some-one" for Jews is possible through the *I am no-one* experience, which reflects Christ's faithfulness and God's universal love for all people, Jews and Gentiles. On the other hand, a problem occurs when Gentile Christians claim that "we are special people of God" (I am some-one) by ignoring the place of Israel in salvation history and treating Jewish laws as futile. Likewise, they assume Jews were abandoned by God because of their unbelief in Christ. But what Gentile Christians fail to understand is God's unsearchable providence or God's mystery that eventually allows for all Israel's salvation (Rom 11:26). All these lead to the importance of faith—faith of Christ, which exemplifies the three moments of life in balance (*I am no-one, I am some-one*, and *I am one-for-others*), as Paul himself identifies with these in his letters (1 Cor 15; 2 Cor 3; Gal 6).

On other occasions in 1 Corinthians, Paul also intervenes when there is no balance between these three modes. Example issues include food offered to idols (1 Cor 8:1–13) and spiritual gifts (1 Cor 14). In 1 Cor 8:1–13, Paul says food is not a matter of importance in faith; however, some people are affected by this knowledge about food. So Paul says: "Therefore, if food is a cause of their falling, I will never eat meat, so that I may not cause one of them to fall" (1 Cor 8:13). Paul's advice is a point of *I am one-for-others*. Sure understanding or a sense of *I am no-one* (understanding of the gospel of Christ) and *I am some-one* (receiving God's love) should point to the third mode of life, *I am one-for-others*.

From the latter case, we can see a similar logic. There is nothing intrinsically wrong when congregants speak in tongues or prophesy when they receive gifts of the Spirit. These are special people (*I am some-one*) and understand the gospel of Christ. Yet, one thing is missing: disregard for fellow congregants when speaking in tongues. This fact suggests that there should be a place of *I am one-for-others*.

Paul's living of *I am one-for-others* is found in his ministry. His living of Christ crucified leads him to various ministry places. Eventually, his ministerial vision extends to Spain as he writes in Romans 15. In Paul's time, Spain is considered by the Roman Empire as resistant and barbarian. The Spanish are considered strange people who deserve only cruelty and control from Rome. But Paul dares to go to this the most barbaric place because in Christ there is no distinction between races or cultures or classes.

Rome is also a place of ministry for Paul even though he did not found any church there. Paul is believed to have met some Roman Jewish Christians elsewhere after they were expelled from Rome in 49 CE (Claudius's edict). A few years later these Roman Jewish Christians returned to Rome and their congregations. Among them are Priscilla and Aquila whom Paul met at Corinth. In that regard, Rome is not unknown to Paul and vice versa. We also know from this letter that he is interested in the Spanish mission and wants to get support from the Roman churches. So in Paul's mind Rome is very important to his mission plan. Rome is the capital of the empire. His involvement with the Roman churches would be symbolically important in that he reaches the center of the empire with his gospel. With Rome's support when he goes on to Spain, Paul would reach the whole world (Spain is considered the end of the world).

A Transformative Reading of the Bible

Throughout his ministry Paul always has all three moments of life balancing his life and ministry. He was never free from his physical weakness or disease (2 Cor 12:7) or from dull speaking or weak bodily presence (2 Cor 10:10). He was never free from misunderstandings from his congregants (1–2 Cor; Gal; Rom). He was never free from persecutions or hardships (2 Cor 4:8–12). He was triply misunderstood by the Gentile Christians (the problem of Gentile arrogance in Romans), Jewish Christians (the problem of ethnocentrism in Romans or Galatians), and nonbelieving Jews (the problem of unenlightened passion for the law in Romans). In the midst of all of these, Paul states that God's grace is enough, and his weakness makes him strong.

Believers' Transformation in 1 Corinthians

The problems of Corinthians may boil down to the issue of power conflict (division, immorality, community, gifts, and resurrection).[5] The majority of Corinthians are from the low class (1 Cor 1:26–30). There are also benefactors or wealthy members in this Corinthian church. There are other strong members, who could boast of their status or special experience (enthusiasts or libertines), spiritual gifts (1 Cor 12–14), or strong knowledge or faith (1 Cor 8). Given this situation at Corinth, members of the Corinthian church are asked to live through three moments of life, as Christ and Paul go through the same cruciform path.

The Importance of I am no-one (1 Cor 1–3)

From the perspective of the lower class, the mode of *I am no-one* represents a miserable status in society and in church, as Paul reminds them: "Consider your own call, brothers and sisters: not many of you were wise by human standards, not many were powerful, not many were of noble birth" (1 Cor 1:26). Many of them are among slaves, or freed slaves, or foreign immigrants who do not have adequate social basis or means to live. These people now hear the gospel of Christ—Christ crucified—from Paul. This gospel is also the gospel of God, who chose the weak and the despised in society. God is the source of new life in Christ Jesus (1 Cor 1:30). Christ's cross gives the message of solidarity to them because Christ suffers with

---

5. Kim, *Christ's Body in Corinth*, 39–63.

them. At the same time, the crucified Christ as a broken body symbolizes their brokenness. If they belong to Christ, they should be like members of Christ in the sense that they treat others better than themselves. They are also "nothing" before God and others.

On the other hand, the mode of *I am no-one* may sound different to the upper class members of the church since they are "special" people in society (and in the church) because of their established name or means of property. But the fact that they joined the church is evidence they are also moved by the message of God's love and Christ's faithfulness, which makes possible a new blessed community of God not on the basis of wealth or birth. The ideas of universal love and moral values could attract some potential leaders in society. It is unikely they joined the church to exercise their power or gain fame, since joining this community of low class people meant risking their honor from the perspective of society. In society upper class people fellowship with their equals. Therefore, it would hardly be the case that a mixed community of the poor and the rich, the weak and the strong, would gather together unless there was common ground between these people (regardless of their place in society). This common ground , for the Corinthian church, could be God's love and Christ's sacrifice. Moved by Christ's unselfish love and sacrifice, these upper class members provide their houses as gathering places for these Corinthians. Gaius, the host of the Corinthian church (1 Cor 1:14), and Erastus, the city treasurer of Corinth (Rom 16:23), are among church members. So the mode of *I am no-one* is understood for these people, as a mode of Christ-like life giving. It is also like Christ's *kenosis* (Phil 2:6–8). These people are not "some-one" because of their social position but because of their participation in the community. Before God's eyes, both the rich and poor are humbled, so they are *I am no-one*.

The Problem of I am some-one (1 Cor 4–11)

But this initial love or mood in the community fades as time goes by, and lots of problems emerge (1 Cor 4–11). Many people claim that they are "special" (*I am some-one*) because of their special experience, knowledge, or faith. This is exactly the problem of Corinthians: claiming the mode of *I am some-one* without involving the modes of *I am no-one* or *I am one-for-others*. The fundamental problem in the Corinthian church is "not to die" (negation of *I am no-one*). Because of this attitude, members of the community fight for their own positions (for example, in the case of food offered to idols or later in cases of spiritual gifts). Denial of *I am no-one* opposes Christ's message of the cross, which accepts death or sacrifice for others even though Jesus is not *I am no-one*. It is an irony to find the fact that while the majority of the Corinthians who were literally "nothing" (no noble birth, education) were chosen by God and became "some-one" as God's children through Christ's cross, they forgot who they were; instead, they try to become *I am some-one* without living the life of nothingness, as Christ did. In other words, the problem is their disembodiment of the Christic body (1 Cor 12:27), as they do not live the gospel of Christ, which embraces the downtrodden and challenges those who do not live up to the law of faith (or the law of God).

The Problem of I am one-for-others (1 Cor 12–14)

First Corinthians 12–14 is concerned with the issue of community. Ideally, the community of Christ should care for each other (as the body analogy implies in chapter 12). Members of the Corinthian community know they are special because of God's love and Christ's faithfulness. Yet one thing is missing: *I am one-for-others*—a true manifestation of love. Even though a person is strong in faith, having knowledge of all mysteries, and even handing over one's body (*I am no-one*), all of these are nothing without love, "a noisy gong or a clanging cymbal" (1 Cor 13:1–3). Here love is an action verb (13:4–8). Love is a leverage point of *I am one-for-others* without which *I am some-one* and *I am no-one* are nothing. Similarly, the problems in chapter 14 are the same in nature. Speaking in tongues is not wrong by itself, and indeed, it is a powerful manifestation of God's work; yet, it should be checked in view of the presence of *others*. The mode of *I am one-for-others* is an important attitude in the life of community. Paul's theology intends that nobody claims the love of God or the faith of Christ without the love of others (neighbors). In this regard, the three loves of political theology work here: the love of self, the love of neighbor, and the love of God.

Conclusion (1 Cor 15–16)

Lastly, believers' transformation looks to the ultimate hope of recovery of God's kingdom. Chapter 15 ensures that the current life of struggle is being transformed and is completed at the end. This hope is apocalyptic and in

A Transformative Reading in Paul's Letters

God's hand. But now transformation is taking place. Chapter 16 reminds the Corinthians that they participate in others' lives. This is also an extension of the mode of *I am one-for-others*. They are being transformed through the act of helping others. So this giving out is not a matter of mercy or mere sharing but a matter of completion, because without giving (or without *I am one-for-others*) there will be an incomplete self, world, and God.

Believers' Transformation in Romans 1–15

Rome's congregations are composed of various social classes.[6] Some churches in Rome, mainly of Jewish upper-class Christians, gather in houses in high-rent areas. Other churches could be supported by benefactors, mainly Gentile patriarchs. Or some churches could gather in low-class urban apartment-like buildings (tenement churches or type of buildings called *insula*). The primary issues facing the diverse congregations in Rome include the relations between Jews and Gentiles, and conflict between different social classes. So given this general situation in Rome, we will see how believers in Rome are asked to go through the process of transformation.

The Importance of I am no-one (Rom 1–3)

Three modes of life appear in balance in Rom 1–3; in it there are important theological claims by Paul. From the beginning of the letter, Paul makes clear that he is "a slave of Jesus Christ (*I am no-one*), called to be an apostle (*I am some-one*), set apart for the gospel of God (*I am one-for-others*)." Through this statement about himself, Paul understands his identity in terms of three moments of life. Paul's work ("for the gospel of God") concerns "his Son, who was descended from David according to the flesh, and was declared to be Son of God with power according to the spirit of holiness by resurrection from the dead" (1:3–4).

These verses, as well, display the three modes of Christ's life: "from the dead" (*I am no-one*), "resurrection from the dead" (*I am some-one*), and "declared to be Son of God with power according to the spirit of holiness" (*I am one-for-others*). "From the dead" signifies all kinds of difficult life experiences, including a moment of death. But Jesus was faithful and God's righteousness is revealed through his faithfulness (Rom 1:17; 3:22),

---

6. Jewett, *Romans*, 1–91.

A Transformative Reading of the Bible

and God's justice or power allows Jesus to be resurrected (*I am some-one*). At the same time, because of his faithfulness, he was "declared to be Son of God with power" and this Son of God serves people with power (*I am one-for-others*).

There are also three modes of life from the audience of Romans. They are called to be saints (*I am some-one*) because of God's grace (*I am no-one before God; I am utterly dependent on God*), and "are called to belong to Jesus Christ" (*I am one-for-others*). "Being called to belong to Jesus Christ" entails Christlike faith and work, which is a life of living for others. Interestingly, Paul (and his coworkers with him) expresses the same faith journey, as he states "through whom (Christ) we have received grace and apostleship to bring about the obedience of faith among all the Gentiles for the sake of his name" (1:5). In this regard, Paul establishes a mutuality with the Romans by sharing the gospel, since the Romans and Paul live the faith journey of three moments in different places. So he mentions that his passion is for the Gentile mission and wants some understanding and support from Romans (1:13–15; 15:23–24).

After this introduction (1:1–15), Paul moves on to clarify the gospel of God and Christ in detail (1:16—3:31). In 1:16–17, the gospel of God is the power of God, which extends salvation to all who have faithfulness of Christ, because salvation is an experience of God's love and radical community of all ("to the Jew first and also to the Greek"), through Christlike faithfulness (1:17; cf. 3:22). Believers participate in this faithfulness of Christ by proclaiming the gospel boldly ("not ashamed of the gospel") because it is the power of God, effective to all people ("through faith for faith" Rom 1:17). In other words, God's righteousness or love can be experienced only when persons live by faith ("the one who is righteous will live by faith" 1:17). This righteousness of God is a manifestation through faith for faith (1:17). First, Christ's faith manifests God's righteousness or love to us, and when we live the same faithfulness, the same righteousness of God is manifested by us. This chain reaction brings in the power of the gospel.

After 1:16–17, Paul further explains why all people, Jews and Gentiles, fall short of God's glory (1:18—3:20). That is because they did not live up to God's will or God's righteousness. Put differently, the problem of all people, Jews or Gentiles, is their disobedience or unfaithfulness. The solution is Christ's faithfulness (3:21–26).

From the language of three moments (modes) of life, we can say the problem of Jews and Gentiles is they do not know who they are (*I am no-one, I am some-one, I am one-for-others*). That is, without honoring God, even though God is revealed in nature or in law, they consider they are *I am some-one* ("claiming to be wise," 1:22), which results in suppressing the truth (1:18). If we truly honor God as God, we should consider "we are no-one" (total dependence on God), then God's power works through us. This is a mode of heteronomy (rule by God).

Similarly, in 2:1–29, if we judge others on the basis of what we know (which is crooked or partial at best because we are mortals before God)—that is, on the basis of *I am some-one* without having the sense of *I am no-one*—the complicated problem is a mode of arrogance, and we may end up imposing our own views onto others. That is what I mean by the problem of "I am one-for-others" in this situation. If Gentile Christians insist that Jews are condemned or their special place is lost because of their unbelief now, it is their overconfidence (*I am some-one*) and arrogance (*I am one-for-others*), because they do not understand who they are (equally sinful and dependent on God's grace, 2:11–12), or they forget that God's love is unmeasured by the human mind or experience ("Do you despise the riches of his kindness and forbearance and patience?" 2:4).

Jews are the same as Gentiles if they claim that *I am some-one* because of their knowledge and confidence in God's law (2:17–29), while not knowing who they are in terms of *I am no-one*. The aggravated problem is also one of arrogance because they teach others with passion (in the mode of *I am one-for-others*) without teaching themselves (2:17–21): "But if you call yourself a Jew and rely on the law and boast of your relation to God and know his will and determine what is best because you are instructed in the law, and if you are sure that you are a guide to the blind, a light to those who are in darkness, a corrector of the foolish, a teacher of children, having in the law the embodiment of knowledge and truth, you, then, that teach others, will you not teach yourself? While you preach against stealing, do you steal?" The conclusion of Romans 2 boils down to the fact that "real circumcision is a matter of the heart—it is spiritual and not literal. Such a person receives praise not from others but from God" (2:29). The solution to the problem of both Jews and Gentiles living in unfaithfulness is Christ's death through which God's righteousness is revealed for all who live the same faith of Christ (3:21–31). If there is any law applicable to Jews and Gentiles, it is "the law of faith" (3:27), which requires three modes of human life in relation to self, neighbor, and God. As Christ sacrificed for others, believers are to do the same.

A Transformative Reading of the Bible

The Problem of I am some-one (Rom 4–8)

The mode of *I am some-one* is affirmation of one's identity. Jews take pride in their possession of the law while Gentiles take pride in new faith in Christ. Each group fights for its own position at the sacrifice of the other. Because of this issue, Paul, in Romans 4, points out the problem of *I am some-one*. Paul says God's promise or love comes first even before faith of Abraham. In other words, it is not because of Abraham's special merits that he deserves God's promise or blessings. From the beginning of Abraham's story in Genesis, it is God's initiative, God's choice of love, and God's granting of posterity. Standing before God, Abraham was *I am no-one* who did not know who God was. He just listens to God and follows what he hears because he is humble. If he were "some-one," he might not have heard God's calling, believing himself to be self-sufficient and not needing God. Abraham's attitude toward himself and God is a mode of *I am no-one* through which God works. In fact, Abraham is a person of the marginalized, an old foreigner, without a child, living on the edge of society as a sojourner before his calling. He probably felt *I am no-one* in this marginalized situation.

Using Abraham as a test case, Paul makes clear that what really matters is faith (or trust) in God, which remains the same from Abraham to the time of Paul. But this faith needs negation of self (*I am no-one*). Put differently, one should affirm one is nothing before God. Only when one affirms he or she is nothing or *no-one*, can one become *some-one*, who walks in love and faith as God's child. When one negates "self" before God, he or she truly sees others; otherwise, what one sees in others is one's own reflection. So in Paul's language, one's baptism means death with Jesus. Then one can live newness of life: "Consider dead to sin and alive to God in Christ Jesus" (6:8–11). Children of God are those who are led by the Spirit and put to death the deeds of the body (8:13).

The Problem of I am one-for-others (Rom 9–11)

In Rom 9–11, the main issue is Gentile arrogance, which is the form of *I am one-for-others* without having a sense of *I am no-one*. When Gentile Christians judge others (Jews) on the basis of the present status (Jews' unbelief) without honoring God's providence or mystery for Israel, they fall into this trap of arrogance. Paul states that we cannot measure God's judgments, wisdom, or knowledge: "O the depth of the riches and wisdom

A Transformative Reading in Paul's Letters

and knowledge of God! How unsearchable are his judgments and how inscrutable his ways! For who has known the mind of the Lord? Or who has been his counselor?" (11:33–34). Gentile Christians can honor of God's mystery when they recognize *I am no-one* before God. Otherwise, their current status as becoming part of God's people (namely, *I am some-one*) leads to arrogance that denies others (Jews). In this way they do not recognize others as God's people. But Paul declares, "all Israel will be saved" (11:26) according to God's providence.

Conclusion: Believers' Transformation in Romans

The picture of balanced transformation that Paul aims at is well expressed in Rom 12:1: "Present your bodies as a living sacrifice, holy and acceptable to God, which is your spiritual worship." "Presenting your bodies" is an act of special service toward God and others. It is done through "a living sacrifice" that requires transformation: "Be transformed by the renewing of your minds" and "discern what is the will of God—what is good and acceptable and perfect" (Rom 12:2).[7] Examples of transformation are shown in the love of others: "Do not think of yourself more highly than you ought to think, but to think sober judgment" (12:3). There are many gifts in the community (12:4–8). Living this other-centered life (*I am one-for-others*) requires radical ethics: "Bless those who persecute you; bless and do not curse them" (12:14); "do not repay anyone evil for evil" (12:17); "if your enemies are hungry, feed them" (12:20).

Paul states that love fulfills the law (13:8). This love is threefold: the love of self, the love of neighbor, and the love of God. If anyone does not welcome the weak (Rom 14–15), there is neither the love of neighbor nor the love of God. The believer should love God through the love of neighbor even when the neighbor is an enemy ("the one who serves Christ is acceptable to God and has human approval," 14:18). This kind of balance is an important trait of a transformed life, as Paul states: "We who are strong ought to put up with the failings of the weak, and not to please ourselves.

---

7. In Romans we see threefold transformation: 1) psychotheological transformation between *I am no-one*, *I am some-one*, and *I am one-for-others*; 2) ontological-theological transformation between autonomy, heteronomy, and relationality; 3) political-theological transformation between self, neighbor, and God. The balance is made between the love of self, the love of neighbor, and the love of God.

A Transformative Reading of the Bible

Each of us must please our neighbor for the good purpose of building up the neighbor. For Christ did not please himself" (15:1–3).

CHAPTER 8

Conclusion

LIFE IN THIS WORLD is unsettling. People want to get out of the difficulty and pain as soon as possible. Nobody wants suffering or pain but the truth is that we cannot avoid it. It may be part of nature. Prince Siddhartha Gautama struggled with this fact of sheer suffering in the world and taught that the solution (salvation) is to let go of all human desires or cares and to enter nirvana—a state of selfless salvation. Similarly, in Hindu tradition, salvation is to dissolve a self so that one can cut the chains of suffering in the next lives (reincarnation) and be united with "the cosmic ultimate, Brahman."[1]

Jewish and Christian traditions differ from the Buddhist or Hindu traditions in the sense that the self is perfected rather than forgotten or dissolved, but their view of suffering as something bad is similar. Wisdom or apocalyptic literature within Jewish tradition understands suffering through the eyes of reward and punishment. The innocent suffering will be rewarded by resurrection while the suffering of the wicked is understood as God's punishment (Dan 12:2–3). Basically, suffering is bad and there is no role of positive human transformation. Even the book of Job, unconventional wisdom literature, struggles with the existence of innocent suffering but does not give an answer to the question of why innocent suffering exists.

The Christian traditions, though complex, generally treat the existence of suffering as bad and look for a new complete world here or beyond this world or this life—a heavenly realm full of peace and joy. On the other hand, in the Taoist tradition of China, suffering or pain is understood as part of a natural world, run by Yin/Yang principles. Simply, good and bad, strong and weak, are necessary and work together in the world. The moon

---

1. Barnes, *In the Presence of Mystery*, 105.

wanes and waxes. "The seed that flowers then withers and drops new seed to the ground."[2] Each season has its distinctive color and taste. In spring, nature turns mild-green; it is a time of hope, and nature and our bodies are full of energy. In summer, our mother nature provides green trees and shade; it is a time of sweat and rest. In fall, nature wears the most beautiful colors; it is a time of joy and reflection. In winter, nature freezes, turning dark and grim; it is a time of preparation for life after winter. These seasonal changes parallel our encounters of the diverse moments in life (hope, love, pain, or suffering).

The concept of human transformation in this book is much like that of the Taoist tradition in certain ways, based on a circular process of human experience rather than on a linear process of upward mobility or on escapism of this world. As nature has an ability to transform itself, we could also. Walking through a trail in a small forest park, I am amazed by the diversity of life: strong and weak trees, standing and fallen trees, tall and small plants, and big rocks and small gravel. All of these live in harmony that consists of both weakness and strength. Nature is transformative because of its adaptability to holistic life. In it, living and nonliving things are not separated but interdependent. In nature there are countless connections of life and each part has its own role or place to be. Likewise, we meet endless changes in our lives, whether they are joy or sorrow, hope or despair. The question is how we use good and bad together for human transformation beyond the dualism between this world and the next world, or between good and bad. The goal of human transformation is to have the right relationship with God, the world (neighbor and enemy), and the self.

The fundamentals of this book are that pain and suffering in the world have a role to play in transformation even if they are bad or unwanted.[3] The apostle Paul chooses the life of pain or suffering for the gospel of Christ. It is not an accident that Paul's sense of calling begins with his difficult life experience—a moment of nothingness: "For *I am the least of the apostles*, unfit to be called an apostle, because I persecuted the church of God. But *by the grace of God I am what I am*, and his grace toward me has not been in vain. On the contrary, *I worked harder* than any of them—though it was not I, but the grace that is with me. Whether then it was I or they, so we proclaim and so you have come to believe" (1 Cor 15:9–11).

---

2. Ibid., 60.

3. Welch, *A Feminist Ethic of Risk*, 93. Welch notes that the important lesson is "how to learn from pain without trying either to conquer it or to become immune to it."

Conclusion

Of course, we need to distinguish between different forms of suffering: (1) some forms of suffering are caused by human evil, (2) some are caused by natural disasters or sickness, and (3) others are caused by voluntary choice. While suffering of human evil is unwanted and is to be resisted, those who suffer because of this are to find the right course of transformation. Similarly, those who suffer due to an unexplainable cause, such as natural disaster, are to find right ways to deal with their suffering. Even those who take suffering by their own choice are to find right ways of dealing with their suffering. Though causes of suffering are different, all this has to do with human transformation because suffering contains a sort of transformative energy within it.

The living and nonliving alike undergo change. Even if we are aware of changes in personhood and in the world, the real lesson that we have to learn is how to respond to each or all changes happening in our lives and the world outside. In this book I propose an alternative model of reading characterized by the threefold transformation: (1) the psychotheological transformation achieved through a balance between "I am no-one," "I am some-one," and "I am one-for-others"; (2) the ontological-theological transformation achieved through a balance between autonomy, heteronomy, and relationality; (3) the political-theological transformation achieved through a balance between the self, neighbor, and God.

Through this nothinglike time, one realizes that he or she is dependent on God and others (friend and enemy) for life. In that sense, dust-made humanity and difficult life experience are not in vain and perhaps celebratory in nature because there is truth in living with limits of not transcending the ordinary life on earth. Put differently, this time of "I am no-one" helps one to understand that his or her life is not self-sufficient but interdependent not only with fellow human beings (including enemies) but with nature and God. An example of our thorough dependence on others or God is clear when we recognize that our life depends on farmers and God together. For example, farmers work hard to grow rice for us; but we know that his or her work would be in vain without the help of nature. To our human life in general this truth might apply: our lives are dependent on others and God. This dependence creates a humble spirit within us that all members of the human community are to be equally cared for.

In the Bible there are many dimensions of story (personal, religious, political) and different genres (history, court records, psalms) composed in different places at different times. Certainly, not all stories in the Bible are

A Transformative Reading of the Bible

equally transformative or helpful. Indeed, some stories are hard to relate to moral transformation. For instance, as we read Jephthah's story in Judges 11:21–40, Jephthah's rash vow costs his young daughter's life. Jephthah swears to God that he will sacrifice as a burnt offering whichever comes first to greet him when he returns from the war in victory. Surprisingly, his daughter comes first to greet him and is sacrificed. Is this episode transformative, holy, and good? Or is it morally blind, and so not transformative? While the answers will vary, the point is that we have to discern what is good and acceptable to God and neighbor. I expect those who are serious about the transformative reading of the Bible to sharpen and deepen my reading of transformation. In the following, I suggest a few tips for a transformative reading.

- Read the story and the entire text as many times as possible to get the overall picture of the story in its diversity and complexity.
- Choose the main character in focus (a figure of transformation) and reread the story back and forth.
- Analyze various life issues and contexts facing this focus-figure of transformation.
- Identify and analyze three moments (modes) of life of the main character.
- Integrate three moments (modes) of life into the larger picture of holistic transformation that involves psychotheological, ontological-theological, and political-theological aspects of life.
- Summarize transformative insights and reflect on your life in view of this transformative reading.

The first step helps readers be familiar with the text or story in historical and literary contexts. As stated earlier, story in the text involves all aspects of life. At this step, it is important to read the story of the text from all angles—from the historical, social, cultural, ideological perspectives. For example, if we focus on the story of Hannah in 2 Sam 2:1–11, we need to study the historical context of Hannah's time, religious and political issues, and her own personal struggle under her social conditions. In addition, an individual story should be also placed in a larger text or literary setting. For instance, Hannah's story can be read in terms of the entire text of 1–2 Samuel. At the second step, as a result of the overall picture of story gained at the first step, we can choose a character that we will focus on. This specific character is usually a person of marginality who goes through various moments of life experience. Once we choose upon whom we will focus, at the third step, we narrow to specific issues faced by the character chosen. For instance, Hannah as a main character of transformation receives full attention, not only from her own life struggle but also from surrounding issues and life conditions of her life such as her family, community, and society. At the fourth step, we have to identify and analyze three moments or modes of life of the main character chosen. The focus will be on how to articulate these moments of life between "I am no-one, I am some-one, and I am one-for-others." The fifth step is an integration mode where the three moments of life can be linked with three subjects of transformation and with three modes of human existence. At this step, hopefully, a summary chart of connections between three modes of human life, three modes of human existence, and three subjects of human transformation will be drawn. The last step is to personalize transformative insights. We may list what we have learned in the process of transformation. The helpful questions are: "Where can I see this kind of transformative story in my life? Or, how can I make a difference with this new transformative perspective in my life?"

Bibliography

Ahn, Jaewoong. *God in our Midst*. Kowloon, Hong Kong: World Student Christian Federation, 1995.
Alter, Robert. *The Art of Biblical Narrative*. New York: Basic Books, 1981.
Althusser, Louis. "Ideology and Ideology State Apparatuses." In *Lenin and Philosophy and Other Essays*, 155–62. Translated by Ben Brewster. New York: Monthly Review, 1971.
Amit, Yairah. "'Am I Not More Devoted to You than Ten Sons?' (1 Samuel 1:8) Male and Female Interpretations." In *A Feminist Companion to Samuel and Kings*, edited by Athalya Brenner, 68–76. Sheffield, UK: Sheffield Academic Press, 1994.
Badiou, Alain. *Saint Paul: The Foundation of Universalism*. Translated by R. Brassier. Stanford: Stanford University Press, 2003.
Barnes, Michael H. *In the Presence of Mystery*. Mystic, CT: Twenty-Third, 2003.
Benjamin, Walter. "The Task of the Translator." In *Walter Benjamin: Selected Writings I*, edited by M. Bullock and M. Jenings, 253–63. Cambridge, MA: Harvard University Press, 1996.
Bultmann, Rudolf. *Der zweite Brief an die Korinther*. KEK 6. Göttingen: Vandenhoeck & Ruprecht, 1976.
Brueggemann, Walter. *First and Second Samuel*. Interpretation. Louisville: John Knox, 1990.
———. *Message of the Psalms: A Theological Commentary*. Minneapolis: Fortress, 1985.
Cartledge, Tony. "Hannah Asked, and God heard." *Review & Expositor* 99/2 (Spring 2002) 143–44.
Chowdhury, A. "Memory, Modernity, Repetition: Walter Benjamin's History." *Telos* 143 (2008) 28–29.
Chung, Hyun Kyung. "'Han-pu-ri': Doing Theology from Korean Women's Perspective." In *Frontiers in Asian Christian Theology*, edited by R. S. Sugirtharajah, 52–62. Maryknoll, NY: Orbis, 1994.
Davies, W. D., and Dale Allison. *The Gospel According to Matthew*. Vol 3. *Matthew 19–28*. ICC. Edinburgh: T&T Clark, 1997.
Derrida, Jacques. "Différance." In *Margins of Philosophy*, 1–27. Translated by Alan Bass. Chicago: University of Chicago Press, 1982.
———. *Negotiations: Interventions and Interviews, 1971–2001*. Stanford: Stanford University Press, 2002.
———. *Of Grammatology*. Translated by Gayatri Chakravorty Spivak. Baltimore: Johns Hopkins University Press, 1974.
———. *The Politics of Friendship*. New York: Verso, 1997.
———. *Positions*. Chicago: University of Chicago Press, 1982.

Bibliography

———. "The Villanova Roundtable." In *Deconstruction in a Nutshell: A Conversation with Jacques Derrida*, edited by John D. Caputo, 1–28. New York: Fordham University Press, 1997.

Dowd, Sharyn, and Elizabeth Malbon. "The Significance of Jesus' Death in Mark: Narrative Context and Authorial Audience." *Journal of Biblical Literature* 125/2 (2006) 271–97.

Dube, Musa W. "'Go Therefore and Make Disciples of All Nations' (Matt. 28:19a) A Postcolonial Perspective on Biblical Criticism and Pedagogy." In *Teaching the Bible*, edited by Fernando Segovia and Mary Ann Tolbert, 224–45. Maryknoll, NY: Orbis, 1998.

Evans, Mary J. *The Message of Samuel: Personalities, Potential, Politics, and Power*. Downers Grove, IL: InterVarsity, 2004.

Freud, Sigmund. *Civilization and Its Discontents*. Translated by James Strachey. New York: Norton, 1989.

Gadamer, Hans-Georg. *A Century of Philosophy*. Translated by Rod Coltman. New York: Continuum, 2003.

Hill, Robert. "St John Chrysostom's Homilies on Hannah." *St. Vladimir's Theological Quarterly* 45/4 (2001) 319–38.

Hopkins, Denise. *Journey through the Psalms*. Christian Board of Publication, 2006.

Hutchison, William R. *Errand to the World: American Protestant Thought and Foreign Missions*. Chicago: University of Chicago Press, 1993.

Janzen, J. Gerald. *Job*. Interpretation. Atlanta: John Knox, 1985.

Jervis, L. Anne. *At the Heart of the Gospel: Suffering in the Earliest Christian Message*. Grand Rapids: Eerdmans, 2007.

Jewett, Robert. *Romans: A Commentary*. Minneapolis: Fortress, 2006.

Kim, Yung Suk. *Biblical Interpretation: Theory, Process, and Criteria*. Eugene, OR: Pickwick, 2012.

———. *Christ's Body in Corinth: The Politics of a Metaphor*. Minneapolis: Fortress, 2008.

———. "Rationale and Proposal for *The Journal of Bible and Human Transformation*." Journal of Bible and Human Transformation 1/1 (November 2011) 1–15. Online: http://www.bibleandtransformation.com/JBHT/Volume_1_(2011)_files/JBHT%201%201%20Kim.pdf.

———. "The Story of Hannah (1 Sam 1:1–2:11) from a Perspective of *Han*: The Three-Phase Transformative Process." *Bible and Critical Theory* 4/2 (2008) 1–9.

———. *A Theological Introduction to Paul's Letters: Exploring a Threefold Theology of Paul*. Eugene, OR: Cascade, 2011.

Kim, Yung Suk, and Jin-ho Kim, eds. *Reading Minjung Theology in the Twenty-First Century: Ahn Byung-Mu's Select Writings and Modern Critical Responses*. Eugene, OR: Pickwick, forthcoming.

Kingsbury, Jack. *Matthew: Structure, Christology, and Kingdom*. Minneapolis: Fortress, 1991.

Klein, Ralph W. *1 Samuel*. Word Biblical Commentary 10. Waco, TX: Word, 1994.

Lacan, Jacques. *The Ethics of Psychoanalysis, 1959-1960*. The Seminar of Jacques Lacan 7. Edited by Jacques-Alain Miller. Translated by Dennis Porter. New York: Norton, 1997.

Lee, Jung Young. *Marginality: The Key to Multicultural Theology*. Minneapolis: Fortress, 1995.

Bibliography

Levinas, Emmanuel. "Dialogue on Thinking-of-the-Other." In *Entre Nous: Thinking of the Other*, 201-6. Translated by Michael B. Smith and Barbara Harshav. New York: Columbia University Press, 1998.

———. *Emmanuel Levinas: Basic Philosophical Writings*. Edited by Adriaan T. Peperzak et al. Bloomington: Indiana University Press, 1996.

———. *Totality and Infinity: An Essay on Exteriority*. Translated by Alphonso Lingis. Pittsburg: Duquesnse University Press, 1969.

Lyman, Stanford M. *The Asian in North America*. Santa Barbara, CA: ABC-Clio, 1977.

Mays, James. "Psalm 13." *Interpretation* 34/3 (July 1980) 279–83.

McCann, J. Clinton. *A Theological Introduction to the Book of Psalms*. Nashville: Abingdon, 1993.

McCarter, K. *1 Samuel*. Anchor Bible 8. Garden City, NY: Doubleday, 1980.

McLaren, Margaret. *Feminism, Foucault, and Embodied Subjectivity*. New York: SUNY Press, 2002.

Meyers, Carol. "The Hannah Narrative in Feminist Perspective." In *Go to the Land I Will Show You: Studies in Honor of Dwight W. Young*, edited by Joseph Coleson and Victor Matthew, 117–26. Winona Lake, IN: Eisenbrauns, 1996.

O'Day, Gail. "Singing Woman's Song: A Hermeneutic of Liberation." *Currents in Theology and Mission* 12/4 (1985) 203–10.

Patte, Daniel, ed. *Cambridge Dictionary of Christianity*. Cambridge: Cambridge University Press, 2010.

———. *The Challenge of Discipleship*. Harrisburg, PA: Trinity International, 1999.

———. *Ethics of Biblical Interpretation: A Reevaluation*. Louisville: John Knox, 1995.

———, ed. *Global Bible Commentary*. Nashville: Abingdon, 2004.

———. *The Gospel of Matthew: A Contextual Introduction for Group Study*. Nashville: Abingdon, 2003.

———. "Reading Matthew 28:16–20 with Others: How It Deconstructs Our Western Concept of Mission." Online: http://www.sbl-site.org/assets/pdfs/Patte_Reading.pdf.

Pereboom, Derk. "Stoic Psychotherapy in Descartes and Spinoza." *Faith and Philosophy* 11 (1994) 592–625.

Reinhard, Kenneth. "Toward a Political Theology of the Neighbor." In *The Neighbor: Three Inquiries in Political Theology*, edited by Slavoj Zizek, Eric L. Santner, and Kenneth Reinhard, 11–75. Chicago: University of Chicago Press, 2006.

Ricoeur, Paul. *Time and Narrative*. Vol. 3. Translated by Kathleen Blamey and David Pellauer. Chicago: University of Chicago Press, 1990.

———. *Oneself as Another*. Translated by Kathleen Blamey. Chicago: University of Chicago Press, 1992.

Santner, Eric L. "Miracles Happen: Benjamin, Rosenzweig, Freud, and the Matter of the Neighbor." In *The Neighbor: Three Inquiries in Political Theology*, edited by Slavoj Zizek, Eric L. Santner, and Kenneth Reinhard, 76–133. Chicago: University of Chicago Press, 2006.

———. *On the Psychotheology of Everyday Life: Reflections on Freud and Rosenzweig*. Chicago: University of Chicago Press, 2001.

Schüssler Fiorenza, Elisabeth. *The Power of the Word: Scripture and the Rhetoric of Empire*. Minneapolis: Fortress, 2007.

———. *Rhetoric and Ethic: The Politics of Biblical Studies*. Minneapolis: Fortress, 1999.

———. *Rights at Risk: Confronting the Cultural, Ethical, and Religious Challenges*. London: Continuum, 2007.

Bibliography

Soares-Prabhu, George. "Two Mission Commands: An Interpretation of Matthew 28:16–20 in Light of a Buddhist Text." In *Voices from the Margins*, edited by R. S. Sugirtharajah, 319–39. Maryknoll, NY: Orbis, 1995.

Stonequist, Everett V. *The Marginal Man: A Study in Personality and Cultural Conflict*. New York: Russell and Russell, 1961.

Suh, Nam-Dong. "Towards a Theology of Han." In *Minjung Theology: People as the Subjects of History*, edited by Yong-bock Kim, 51–65. Singapore: Christian Conference of Asia, 1981.

Tamez, Elsa. *Bible of the Oppressed*. Maryknoll, NY: Orbis, 1982.

Wainwright, Elaine M. *Shall We Look for Another: A Feminist Rereading of the Matthean Jesus*. Maryknoll, NY: Orbis, 1998.

Welborn, Laurence L. "Extraction from the Mortal Site: Badiou on the Resurrection in Paul." *New Testament Studies* 55 (2009) 295–314.

———. "Paul and Pain: Paul's Emotional Therapy in 2 Corinthians 1.1—2.13; 7.5–16 in the Context of Ancient Psychagogic Literature." *New Testament Studies* 57 (2011) 547–70.

Welch, Sharon D. *A Feminist Ethic of Risk*. Minneapolis: Fortress, 2000.

Westermann, Claus. *Praise and Lament in the Psalms*. Louisville: Westminster John Knox, 1981.

Wimberly, Edward P. *Prayer in Pastoral Counseling: Suffering, Healing and Discernment*. Louisville: Westminster John Knox, 2000.

Wink, Walter. *The Bible in Human Transformation*. Philadelphia: Fortress, 1973.

———. *The Human Being: Jesus and the Enigma of the Son of the Man*. Minneapolis: Fortress, 2001.

———. *Transforming Bible Study*. Nashville: Abingdon, 1989.

Zizek, Slavoj, Eric L. Santner, and Kenneth Reinhard, eds. *The Neighbor: Three Inquiries in Political Theology*. Chicago: University of Chicago Press, 2006.

Subject Index

A

Abraham, 67–68, 80
Adam, 31n13
afterlife, 31n13
Agamben, Giorgio, 15
Allison, Dale, 5
Amit, Yairah, 41, 42n26
arrogance, 67, 74, 79–81
Augustine, 18, 38n2
autonomy, xvi, 3–13, 22, 27–28, 31–33, 36, 45, 52, 81, 85

B

Badiou, Alain, 15, 19
balance, ix, xiv, xvi, 10–11, 21–22, 27, 31, 34, 36, 46–47, 69, 72–73, 77, 81, 85
baptism, 59–63, 80
Benjamin, Walter, 19
Brown, Raymond, 7n13
Brueggemann, Walter, 38n3, 49–50

C

caution (*eulabeia*), 20
Caesar, 62
Christ crucified, 68–70, 73–74
Christic body, 76
Chrysostom, 38n2
Claudius' edict, 73
complexity, 86
Corinthians, 67–68, 73–77

creation, 26–27, 31n13, 40n20, 54, 68–70
creatureliness, 54
cross, 5–6, 18–20, 30–31, 59, 63–65, 68–70, 72, 74, 76

D

Dante, 31n13
darkness, 8n14, 14, 17n11, 22, 28, 50, 53–55, 79
David, 77
Dasein, 24
Davies, W.D, 5
deontological view, 5
Derrida, Jacques, 13, 15
determination, xvi, 41, 55–56
dikaiosyne theou, 72
disorientation, 50
diversity, 12–13, 84, 86
Dube, Musa, 6n11, 7n12

E

Egypt, 33n14
Eli, 41–42, 44
Elkanah, 41–43
embodiment, 79
enemy, 3, 14–16, 25–26, 29, 31n13, 34–35, 48–56, 81, 84–85
engagement, xvi, 17n11, 25–26, 28–29, 33n14, 44, 52–53, 55–57
enlightenment, 4, 12–13, 28
Erastus, 75
ethnocentrism, 62, 74

Subject Index

experience, xi, xv–xvi, 3, 6–9, 15, 17n11, 18–19, 23–32, 39–45, 48–50, 52, 55, 60–61, 64, 66–80, 84–87

F

faith, xii–xiii, 7, 17n11, 21, 29, 38n2, 49–50, 53–54, 56–57, 64–80
faithfulness, 18, 67–68, 72, 75–79
fantasies, 21, 30
fear (*phobos*), 20
First Jewish Revolt, 58
freedom, 6, 17n11
Freud, Sigmund, 3, 13–16, 23, 25, 50
friend, 15–16, 25–26, 29, 35, 85

G

Gadamer, Hans-Georg, 24n6
genre, 61, 85
Gentiles, 63–65, 68, 72, 77–80
Gentile Christians, 58, 72, 74, 79–81
godly grief, 20
God's law, 21, 79
Good news (or *euangelion*), xv, 58–66
grace of God, 66, 68, 84
Greek Orthodox tradition, 8
Gulf of Mexico, 54

H

han, 39n10, 41–47
Hannah, xii–xvii, 29–30, 37–47
Harrington, Daniel, 7n13
Heidegger, Martin, 24
heteronomy, xvi, 3–15, 22, 27, 31–33, 36, 45, 52, 54, 64, 79, 81n7, 85
heteronomous autonomy, 45
Holistic Model, xviii, 4, 9–10
hope, 17–19, 26–27, 39, 41, 52–53, 54–57, 76, 84
human attitude, xv–xvi, 21, 61
human existence, 3–4, 6–14, 22, 27, 31–32, 33n14, 34, 36, 87

human life, xv–xvi, 3, 6, 10–16, 21, 26–27, 31–32, 34, 37, 50, 53, 79, 85, 87

I

immanent transcendence, xv
Isaiah, 28, 61
Israel, 7n13, 62–63, 68, 72, 80–81

J

Jephthah, 86
Jerusalem Temple, 8n14
Jervis, L., 18
Jewish Christians, 73–74
Jews, 64–65, 68, 72, 74, 77–81
Job, 17, 43n29, 83
joy (*chara*), 20
Judaism, 67–68
Judges, 86
justice, 1, 6–7, 12–3, 21, 55–57, 60, 64–65, 78

K

Kant, Immanuel, 12–15
kenosis, 75
Kim, Yung Suk, 13n4, 38n1, 67n1, 69n4, 74n5
Kingdom of God, 13n4, 18–19, 59, 63
kyriarchy, 2

L

Lacan, Jacques, 16
lament, 48–55
lament psalms: personal, 48; communal, 48, 55
Last Supper, 60, 63
law, 8n14, 18, 21, 68–69, 72, 74, 76, 79–81
Lee, Jung Young, 39–41
Levinas, Emmanuel, 13n1, 25, 45n31
Liberation Model, 4, 6–7

Subject Index

loneliness, 23, 53
loss, 20–21, 29–30, 69
lype, 20

M

Mark (Gospel of), xiii, 37, 58–66
Markan community, 60, 64–66
Markan Jesus, 60, 62
Matthew (Gospel of), 5–8
Mays, James, 49–50
McCann, J. Clinton, 49n5
Messiah, 7n13, 13n4, 61, 68
metaethical self, 23, 25
metanoia (or *metanoeo*), xiii
minjung theology, 13n4
Moses, 33n14

N

nature, 26, 30, 70, 79, 83–5
neighbor, xiv–xvi, 3, 10–11, 14–16, 22–26, 28–29, 31–32, 34–37, 46–49, 57, 76, 79, 81–82, 84, 86
neben, 54
nefesh, 27–28, 40n20, 44, 56
Nero, 58, 64
new orientation, 50
Nietzsche, Friedrich, 12–3
nothingness, 14, 17n11, 19, 22–23, 26–29, 41, 44–46, 53–54, 65, 71, 76, 84
nuclear fission, 29
nuclear fusion, 30

O

orientation, 50
overconfidence, 79

P

pain, 15, 17–18, 20–3, 25–30, 41, 43, 50–3, 56–7, 83–84
passion, 74, 78–79
Patte, Daniel, 2, 5–6

Paul's letters, 18, 37, 67, 69
Paul's theology, 18, 19n13, 20, 30, 69n4, 76
Peter, xiv, 8n13, 58, 65
petros, 8n13
pistis christou, 72
pleasure (*hedone*), 20
political theology, 2–3, 11, 14, 16, 25, 29–30, 34–36, 76
powerlessness, 41, 52–54
prayer, 28–29, 38, 45–46, 52, 56, 60
promise, 67, 80
Psalm 13, 37, 48–57
psychological lump, 15
psychotheology, 2–3, 11, 14n5, 23n3, 24n7
psychotherapy, xv, 15, 20n17, 25
punishment, 17–18, 31n13, 48, 55, 83

Q

queshat ruah, 44
Qumran community, 8

R

Reinhard, Kenneth, 3, 15–16
relational self, 36
relationality, 3–13, 22–23, 27, 31–33, 36, 52, 81n7, 85
relationless relation, 13
Religious Community Model, 4, 7, 9
Religious Individual Model, 4, 9
repentance, 20
Ricoeur, Paul, 13n1, 39n11
righteousness, 21, 56–57, 64, 67–72, 77–79
Roman Catholic tradition, 8
Romans, 30, 67–68, 70, 72–74, 77–81
Rome, 58, 64–65, 73, 77
Rosenzweig, Franz, 3, 14, 23, 25, 54

S

sacrifice, 10, 12, 29–30, 64, 70, 72, 75–76, 80–81, 86

95

Subject Index

Samuel, 30, 38, 42, 45–46, 86
Santner, Eric, 3, 14, 23n3, 24–25
Satan, 59, 62
Schüssler Fiorenza, Elisabeth, 2
Secret Sunshine, 34
sheol, 44
shub, xiii
Siddhartha Gautama, 83
sin, 17–18, 21, 27
Soares-Prabhu, George, 7n12
social change, 6
solidarity, 31, 74
Son of God, 58–59, 61–64, 66, 77–78
Son of Man, 66
spiritual gifts, 73–74, 76
Stoics, 20
story, 16, 29, 37–47, 53–54, 6–72, 80–87
subjective genitive, 72
suffering, 15, 17–18, 20–22, 25–28, 38, 40, 43, 49, 51–66, 69–73, 83–85
superego, 23
Syro-Phoenician woman, 63
system of reward and punishment, 17

T

thanksgiving, 55–56
three loves, 16, 76
threefold theology, 69n4
transformative: experience, 31, 60, 67, 69; identity, 39–40; perspective, 87; story, xii, 87
transforming power, xiii–xv
transformation: human, 1–6, 10–16, 18–20, 22–26, 29, 31, 36, 83–85, 87; holistic, 11, 21–22, 37, 57, 86; personal, 48–49, 52; public, 46; threefold, 35–36, 81n7, 85; psychotheological, 27, 31, 81n7, 85; ontological-theological, 27, 32, 34–36, 81n7, 85; political-theological, 27, 34–35, 81n7, 85; charismatic, 4, 9; cycle, 27–28, 37
Torah, 31n13
trust, 49, 51–53, 55
tsedaka, 57

U

Usual Western Model, 4, 6, 8, 9
Utopia, 31

V

volition (*boulesis*), 20

W

Wainwright, Elaine, 7n12
Welborn, Laurence, 19, 20n18
Welch, Sharon, 21n19, 23n2, 84n3
Wimberly, Edward, 28
Wink, Walter, 1, 2n1

Y

Yin/Yang, 83

Z

Zizek, Slavoj, 3, 15

www.ingramcontent.com/pod-product-compliance
Lightning Source LLC
Chambersburg PA
CBHW020207090426
42734CB00008B/974